"Our lives have the potential, in the words of Dom Gregory Dix, to 'take the shape of the liturgy.' In Ryan Snider's imaginative work, we discover that God's story is our story, that worship is more than Sunday morning, and that in community, we become more human. A wonderful and sustained reflection on identity and purpose!"

—**Bishop Ken Carter,** United Methodist Church, author of 18 books, including *God Will Make a Way*

"Ryan Snider's new book, *Ancient Extravagance*, aims at what many Christians badly want and need: a deeply Christian expression of our God-given humanity. That expression is imbedded in the ordered worship of God's people. Snider encourages us by means of storied reflections and reflective stories toward a 'better way' of living the life God intended for all of us. This is an inspiring book."

—**Richard Lischer,** author of *Our Hearts Are Restless: The Art of Spiritual Memoir*

"Ryan's voice is winsome, wise, and kind. He brings academic theology into a more accessible place."

—**Jason Byassee,** Timothy Eaton Memorial Church, Toronto, Ontario, author of *Northern Lights*, *Better than Brunch*, and *Surprised by Jesus Again*

"I was fortunate to read this book and was delighted at how Ryan turns his thoughts into language—he's a strong storyteller. Through his writing, it is clear he shoulders a love and concern for the aims and practices of the church, and as a pastor in his family's parish, these burdens are obvious in his life and engagement with his own faith community."

—**Derek Sweatman,** Atlanta Christian Church, author of articles in *Mockingbird* and *Christianity Today*

"At first glance this is a deeply humane book that builds on our life experience and demonstrates how the Holy Spirit turns it from water into wine. But on closer inspection this is a profoundly incarnate book that inspires us through example, argument, anecdote, and timely quotation to see God in Christ entering the intricacies of our mundane existence and raising up that existence into the heart of God's eternal essence. As you read you will find the exalted in your life humbled and the humble in your life exalted."

—**Samuel Wells,** Vicar of St Martin-in-the-Fields, Trafalgar Square, London

ANCIENT
EXTRAVAGANCE

ANCIENT
EXTRAVAGANCE

Christian Ways of Becoming More Human

RYAN SNIDER

LEAFWOOD
PUBLISHERS
an imprint of Abilene Christian University Press

ANCIENT EXTRAVAGANCE
Christian Ways of Becoming More Human

an imprint of Abilene Christian University Press

Copyright © 2024 by Ryan Snider

ISBN 978-1-68426-083-6

Printed in the United States of America

ALL RIGHTS RESERVED
No part of this publication may be reproduced, stored in a retrieval system, or transmitted in any form by any means—electronic, mechanical, photocopying, recording, or otherwise—without prior written consent.

Scripture quotations, unless otherwise noted, are taken from the New Revised Standard Version Bible, Updated Edition, NRSVUE, copyright © 2021 the Division of Christian Education of the National Council of the Churches of Christ in the United States of America. Used by permission. All rights reserved.

Scripture quotations noted *The Message* taken from The Message. Copyright © 1993, 1994, 1995, 1996, 2000, 2001, 2002. Used by permission of NavPress Publishing Group.

Cataloging-in-Publication Data is on file at the Library of Congress, Washington, DC.

Cover design by Greg Jackson, Thinkpen Design
Interior text design by Sandy Armstrong, Strong Design

Leafwood Publishers is an imprint of Abilene Christian University Press
ACU Box 29138
Abilene, Texas 79699

1-877-816-4455
www.leafwoodpublishers.com

24 25 26 27 28 29 30 // 7 6 5 4 3 2 1

For Mom and Dad. Thanks for the stories.

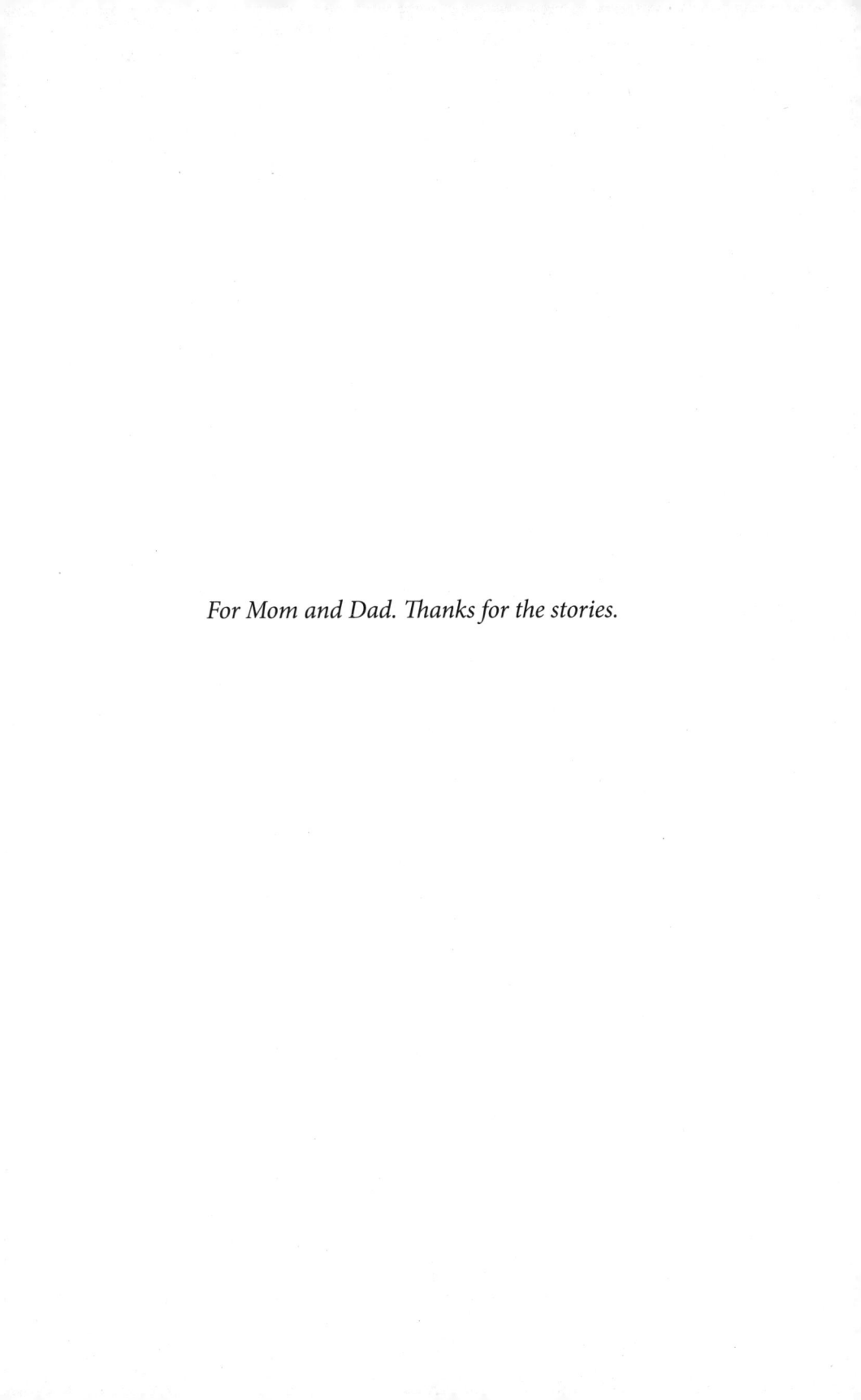

CONTENTS

Prelude········11
Wasteful Words········17

ONE
GATHERING

You Have Been Welcomed········25
Embraced by Family and Friends········29
At Home in Body and Spirit········41

TWO
BEAUTY

Singing Is Who We Are········51
Cross-Shaped Pictures········61
Singing Who We Will Be········71

THREE
SACRED STORIES

A Genesis: Our First Stories········79
Seventy Faces of the Torah: Reading the Story········89
Touching the Gospel: Living the Story········97
Prodigal, Extravagant Love: Sharing the Story········105

INTERLUDE
WASTED TIME

The Longest, Shortest Time········111
Evening, Morning—A Day········117
A Moment of Silence········121
A Week········123

FOUR
GOD AND TABLES

Setting the Table: You Are What You Eat ·········· **141**
Thanksgiving: Noticing the Blessings ·········**145**
Anamnesis: Re-membering Christ ·········· **151**
Take, Bless, Break, Give: Extending the Table ·········· **161**

FIVE
GOD'S
EXTRAVAGANT GRACE

A Baptism: Called Beloved ·········· **169**
Confession of Doubt: Holding on When There's Nothing to Believe ·········· **177**
Prayer: Pestered by God ·········· **185**

BENEDICTION

Watching the Tides ·········· **193**
Following God's (Ordinary) Call ·········· **199**
Planted in New Soil ·········· **211**

Epilogue: Sending Forth ·········· **221**
Acknowledgments ·········· **231**
Notes ·········· **233**

Prelude

We are all frittering away our lives—at least according to someone. I must not be the only one constantly bombarded with people, advertisements, and street preachers telling me not to waste my life. Every culture, faith, and person has an idea about a wasted life because they have an idea of the contents of a good life. There is no wasted life without an ideal life. Implicit in every story is a worldview or understanding of the world telling you exactly what is most valuable. Life is meant to be lived toward a particular end; when it's not, it's wasted.

The market, for instance, describes the good life through consumerism and the accumulation of goods—a capitalistic theory of goodness founded on success, acquisition, and consumption. Unsettled with the present, we work to be somewhere else. We know we will be happier if we make more money or buy a nicer car and a bigger house. We exist to consume. This is why our country is one of the most wasteful—fast fashion, the maximization of our time, the commoditization of cheap food. A former professor of mine mentioned that most Americans envision the world as a warehouse.[1] "We'll buy another" is our motto. We end up wasting a lot of stuff to avoid wasting our lives.

An alternative theory of the good life is described by the accumulation of experiences, with travel and places to see before we die. The goal is to retire early so you can make the most of life with bucket lists and inordinate amounts of adventures. Think of the people who will take a last-minute flight to a resort in Cancun for the weekend. Is there anything more annoying? Confession: It's only annoying because I have kids. And because I don't have money. Since that's the case, it's a waste of time, resources, and greenhouse gases.

Thanks for destroying our planet.

Even still, another theory of a good life might argue that contentment comes from within by developing inner tranquility and acceptance; happiness will not arise from making the world conform to your desires. The more you desire and attach, the likelier you are to suffer. The objective of the good life is to focus on what you can control without letting external circumstances define your life. Learn to live within your boundaries.

Which theory of the good life do you buy into?

The stories that shape our identity and purpose aren't usually obvious—this is to say, they aren't always read from a book or proclaimed from a podium. Instead, they are subtly flashed across a screen before your feet meet the carpet in the morning. These images invite our hearts to envy as we compare ourselves to another's highlight reel. It's the smile or frown of our parents after we've made a life-changing decision. We are taught about the good life from products that can be attained cheaply and immediately, with the click of a button, divorcing their production from people and places, all the while training us to desire consumption. Think of the enacted rituals or behaviors you must engage in to "belong" to a particular group. These practices and encounters shape our hearts and imaginations, forming our desires toward a specific vision of the good life.[2]

The question we must ask ourselves is this: Is there a better story about the good life?

Many have heard the oft told story about thieves who broke into a jewelry store and didn't steal anything; they simply rearranged the price tags.[3] The next morning, the expensive jewelry was sold as junk, a Rolex for a Timex. And the junk was sold as expensive jewelry. In the morning, they watched with delight as people walked out with Rolex watches for the price of Timex pieces.

Value is constantly being rearranged as we are taught what to desire and pursue. If you control a person's desires, then you control the person.

And we're constantly being subjected to the formation of our desires—the narratives, the advertisements, the media, the politics that form our hearts and shape our imaginations and assumptions about the "good life." But we rarely take enough time to reflect on the stories that have worked their way into our subconscious, replacing and shaping the stories that we know are most beautiful and valuable. Instead, we rush to the cashier with the things that won't stand the test of time—a sweater that will wear down after a season's use.

Martin Luther said, "Wherever your heart is, there is your God." What do we really long for? Where do we spend our time, money, energy, and resources? Wherever that is, that's what we worship. We fool ourselves when we believe we don't worship anything. David Foster Wallace puts it this way:

> There is no such thing as not worshipping. Everybody worships. The only choice we get is what to worship.... If you worship money and things... then you will never have enough. Never feel you have enough. It's the truth. Worship your own body and beauty and sexual allure and you will always feel ugly, and when time and age start showing, you will die a million deaths before they finally plant you.[4]

To worship is to ascribe worth—and we all ascribe worth to something. Wallace argues that the object of our worth defines us. To worship is to inhabit a set of desires worth pursuing; it's to receive a destination, a place of human flourishing, at the expense of all others. In other words, we all become what we worship.[5]

Groups of people have asked me why I'm still a Christian. Worshipping God can feel like a complete waste of time (depending on what god you're following). When you go to a Christian worship service, you cease all useful and productive activity for the better part of an hour. Enter the building, make small talk about Braves baseball, sing a few songs, read old stories, listen to a message, leave. Oh yeah, you might get to eat Jesus's body every few weeks. And when it's really good, we dunk people in water.

Presumably, the hour didn't do much for your life, much less the common good of society. Worship is a bit like nineties television. Usually average. Almost always forgettable. If you caught it, you caught it. If you didn't, they'll air something mediocre next week. That's why it's increasingly tempting to wake up, smell that coffee, and remain in your pajamas. Life is busy. You can get more done if you stay home. I've heard that voice before too. Just stream a sermon or a podcast that's tailored to your needs and desires. Read a book, maybe. Then, the leaves will get raked, groceries bought, and you'll still have time to catch the Falcons game.

But something happens when we sing praises, open Scripture, or pray for God's Spirit to descend upon our lives. Worship is not simply talking and singing about God but meeting and communing with the living God through the risen Christ in the power of the Holy Spirit. Dietrich Bonhoeffer says Christ actually walks up and down the aisles each and every time the Word is proclaimed.[6] And most Sundays, something does happen—through us, despite us, beyond us—you'll encounter God. But even if you are just going through the motions, know this: The weekly habits of praise, thanksgiving, confession, peace, and grace will change your life, whether you realize it or not. The practices of worship, like welcoming and sharing food, shape our imagination of our lives and world, which then shapes our character and the kind of people we become. In other words, we are immersed in rituals that train us to love.

Marva Dawn has a book about worship called *A Royal Waste of Time*. She's right. Christianity offers an alternative, less sexy theory about life; it doesn't promise power, money, or stuff. All it can offer is God and neighbor. Christianity, at the core, is a religion of wasteful love. My favorite word to describe Christianity, therefore, is "prodigal." To be *prodigal* is to be extravagantly wasteful, profligate, reckless—to throw away a life. It's there, I promise, even if you have to peer behind the carefully rehearsed worship, Excel budget sheets, and strategic plans.

Christianity is wasteful in the best sense. A life formed by worship, I believe, is more beautiful than anything I could manufacture on my own. When I'm left to my own devices, I'm susceptible to the three temptations that have always plagued humanity: success, relevancy, and power.[7] But the purpose of Christian worship is the enterprise of putting the price tags of our lives in a better order. Worship changes our longings so that we start to share God's values of hospitality, beauty, thanksgiving, and, most of all, love. In an increasingly post-Christian society, Christian practices can provide a counter-witness to a world obsessed with shallow consumption, anxious efficiency, and violence to oneself and neighbor.

In the following chapters, I will follow a traditional order of worship, moving from gathering to benediction, or being sent. The pattern of our worship mirrors the way of God's movement in our lives: We gather, we encounter, we respond, and we are sent. The rituals and practices of our worship form us into a kind of people who inhabit the world differently. These practices start small—with a person or a family, a handshake, a splash of water, a song, a family meal. But each practice of worship is a mustard seed that, when planted, will create shade for the whole world.

The Christian hope is that one day, there will be worship of God without end. That doesn't mean you will be subjected to a never-ending sermon. Instead, you'll be perfected in the love of God, creation, and one another. Christians rehearse for that end as the fulfillment of this life. Weekly. At least. After all, if we get enough reps in, worship might eventually become an instinct—your life might become a foretaste of heaven on earth.

Rabbi Abraham Heschel once noted that people complained that their worship was boring and rote. They were sick of doing the same things each week. Heschel responded, "Have you become the worship yet?" And they looked confused.

"When you become the worship, that's when we can stop doing it."

Instead of going to worship, you become the worship.

Your life becomes wasteful, or extravagant, in love.

Wasteful Words

I never liked poetry. I didn't understand the haphazard spacing, nonsensical capitalization, and pretentious depth. Hope is not "the thing with feathers," contrary to Emily Dickinson's opinion. Poetry has to be one of the most wasteful ways of communication. There is rhythm, I know, but what's the point? There is a clearer, more economical way to discuss hope without all the adjectives and metaphors. Here's one: Hope is when the world has gone to hell, but you still act like it hasn't. I'm not sure if that has feathers or not.

Many people have tried to teach me to read throughout my life, but none prepared me to read so that I could value poetry. It began in grade school when I was forced to take Accelerated Reader tests and reach a certain point quota. I read *Moby Dick* in second grade. Not the full-length novel, of course. I found the Great Illustrated Classics edition, an adaptation of the story with a big typeface and illustrations. Give me the whale without all the tedious waiting and fishing. I got Herman's gist and took the test for thirty-something points. Quota met.

Later, I started a little business by taking tests for my classmates—one dollar per test. It was the first and last entrepreneurial moment of my life.

In high school, my first-year English class realized someone had already compiled all the themes of *Great Expectations* in a yellow-and-black striped book—Cliff's Notes. Why slog through five hundred pages to learn about social class? Someone had compiled all the themes and motifs with neat headlines. I could consume the information in half an hour.

College professors later taught me about efficient reading: "Good writers will frame their work with topic sentences and conclusions. Read the conclusion first and then the introduction. Read the first and last sentence of each paragraph. Follow the bread crumbs, designated by the words 'in sum,' and you'll get what you need." And most of the time, it worked; if "working" meant separating the kernel from the husk to pass the test or write the paper.

And so poetry is a waste of time unless it's based on something other than Accelerated Reader points, gists, and summaries.

I didn't really learn how to read in graduate school. I was taking a class on the Gospel of Luke, and our first assignment was to read the entire Gospel in one sitting—nine separate times. I did the work because I'm anxious by nature and have spent my life trying to overachieve. I didn't understand why we spent the first two weeks of class without reading the commentaries written by experts—you know, the kinds of people who could tell us what the text actually meant.

Worse, the professor didn't answer any of our questions as we posed them in class. What does it mean, I wondered, that this second-century Messiah told us to sell all our things and give the money to the poor? Surely, this was hyperbolic, like when Jesus told us to turn the other cheek. This professor shrugged his shoulders or, like a gadfly, asked a more difficult question. I needed the answer so I could write it in my notebook, memorize it for the test, and belittle my classmates in the process (graduate school is the place where knowing all the answers makes you cool—the bullies wore tweed jackets and could shoot you dead with a theology bullet from an obscure theologian).

I wasn't sure why he was getting paid.

It took an entire semester for me to realize I hadn't wasted a few thousand dollars. Our professor was trying to show us that education, especially theology, isn't about acquiring information, though that can be important; instead, the formation of a person is more crucial. If you're striving to become the master of the narrative, then you've got it all backward. The narrative exists as a means for God to change you. The question that mattered at the end of the semester was this: Were we looking at the world through Luke's eyes? If we were, we would have encountered Jesus, and our professor would have done his job.

Most of us must be retaught to read, especially in an age of mass information. The shift from the printed word to the pixel word has trained readers to skim the surface, separating the wheat from the chaff. With artificial intelligence, our culture is on the verge of injecting information into our brains through the same machines utilized in *The Matrix*. But reading well means not rushing through the words to get to the point and collect the information. Instead, reading well is about taking time to dwell with words so that we might learn to dwell in the world—especially with others. After all, the instrumentalization of someone's words is a form of instrumentalizing people. Can we see the world through another person's eyes, encounter Jesus, and thus become a new kind of person?

One way to practice this is by reading with a presumption of innocence and a premise of grace. I often come to the written page with suspicion rather than charity; my guards are raised. This is especially true if someone writes about God, politics, or sports, the three great religions in our culture. Some suspicion is natural when your identity, communities, and beliefs are at stake. I am primed and ready to look for holes, inconsistencies, and logical fallacies.

I remember the first time I had to read John Calvin, who I knew was my mortal enemy in graduate school. I grew up Methodist and knew we had certain theological friends and foes. Moravians were in our camp, as were the Anglicans and Arminians. On the other hand, Calvin thought God was a cranky, controlling monarch (my words). There was no room for him, even though the founder of Methodism was great friends with plenty of Calvinists. And then I read some of the stuff Calvin actually wrote about idolatry, and I began to give him grace even though he was a little stingy with the stuff.

Critiquing is easy; looking for beauty is much more difficult. And much more rewarding. A hermeneutic of charity means approaching the text with two presuppositions: First, you could be wrong. Yes, even you. Christianity is all about repentance, which means you might consider the ways you are wrong and begin to walk in a new direction. And second, you always have something to learn. Yes, even from your mortal enemy. Reading well is when you encounter another person's truth and wrestle with it before you dismiss it. It's a hard pill to swallow in a polarized and tribal world, but it can be done. Just remember that you once heard about a Methodist who sometimes quotes the person who believes God predestines people to hell.

You'll be better for this, I promise. When you come across a rational argument challenging a well-held belief, you'll be pressed to clarify your beliefs or change your mind. Either way, you grow. So much of what changes our lives comes from outside our narrow window of the world. What's more is that you'll learn you don't have to completely agree with another person to commune with them—kind of like Mathew, Mark, Luke, and John. The Gospels seem to have fairly different portraits of Jesus, but they commune together pretty nicely. Even more, the conversation between the four accounts elicits a richer encounter with God.

All this is to say that how we read says something about the kind of human being we want to become. Our fractured world depends on us learning to become better readers. The "people of the Book" ought to be up for the challenge. Thus, we ought to practice reading charitably and extravagantly.

In this book, I will convey ideas and information, but it will not be a systematic theology of worship. This book is less about consuming information. You can understand the principles of something and not be changed. That's why there are also stories, images, and poems. A story helps us release God out of our brains, if only for a minute, and let the Spirit seep into our hearts and bones as our senses override the intellect. Poems won't necessarily make you smarter, a great theologian, or the best at "sword drills." But they might help you exchange knowing for being and, thus, slow down, pay attention, and dwell in beauty.

In other words, if I wanted you to bank information, then I'd give you headers and memorizable points. But since I'd rather that you encounter God and yourself, I'm telling you stories (note, particularly, the "Sacred Stories" section that is almost entirely comprised of a collage of stories; much like our own lives, we must stitch together the stories to make a comprehensive whole). There are better books to help you become a more astute theologian, but this one might help you realize how the Christian life can be beautiful.

A careful reader who is steeped in the tradition of the church will notice that the chapters are based on a traditional order of worship. Each chapter, then, is a creative way of exploring what we're doing in worship. You will grab a cup of coffee when you're welcomed, sing a song of preparation and response, read from the Torah and the Gospels, share in the liturgy of the Lord's Table, and respond with prayer, baptism, and faith or doubt. All this happens before you are sent away. I show why these rituals are important and how they continue to shape my life. I hope that it's interesting. But more importantly, my biggest hope is that you'll juxtapose the beauty I have experienced in my life with the beauty that lingers in your heart.

Reading slowly can sharpen our attention to see the world differently. When I waste a few words, I'm writing with the assumption that life is meant to be lived with a bit of extravagance. Can we learn to dwell on a paragraph, a word, or a letter instead of rushing to the next page? Wasteful words might not be efficient, but they might just help you live an extravagant life.

ONE

GATHERING

You Have Been Welcomed

Three years old is a bit premature for a first existential crisis. My daughter spotted a picture of my wife from middle school while we were visiting her Yaya and Grandpa. In the photo, my wife was sandwiched between her two brothers, all looking noticeably younger.

"Where was I?" said Eden.

Kids say cute things and ask complicated and annoying questions that we don't think of or want to ask, almost always at the most inconvenient times possible. Kids are observant, but they're also gauche and socially undiscerning. Are we really going to get into ontology at eight in the morning? Read the room.

Someone once asked Augustine about preexistence: "What was God doing before he made heaven and earth?" Augustine replied, "He was preparing Hell for people who pry into mysteries."[1] That's as good an answer as any, but unfortunately, it's inappropriate for my three-year-old daughter. What does one say about preexistence and postexistence to those just now encountering their own existence? Young children (and also many adults) are so egocentric that they have difficulty perceiving a world that doesn't contain them.

"Well, you weren't born yet," one of us responded. I'm not sure whether it was my wife or me. It doesn't matter. Small kids are concrete thinkers. Best to say as little as possible. Eden's head dropped, and little wrinkles formed around her eyes. She squinted in confusion.

"You were with the stars," we said.

Look, save your critique. Parenting ought to be a judgment-free zone—especially before coffee. We knew it was not right, but it's not terribly wrong. Aren't we all just stardust, anyway? It's cliché and sentimental, and she's a three-year-old who can't read.

It didn't work.

"I was in the dark? Alone? I don't want to be in the dark!"

Complete meltdown.

Here's what's worse: I caught her drawing pictures of herself in the stars a couple of weeks later. It was a portrait of hell—an existence that's only dark. A life that's only isolation. I asked her how it felt to be with the stars.

She said two words: "It's sad." (So much for the soothing lull of "Twinkle, Twinkle, Little Star.")

There's a better answer to these questions of existence and nonexistence, though Eden was too young to grasp it. It's this: You were created. You were given a beginning, just as there was an initial beginning to all things. It's a miracle that there is something rather than not-something; it's more miraculous that there is conscious life and an even greater miracle that there is someone like you.

Or maybe it's not. God is self-determined and resolved to be Creator. Not out of compulsion, necessity, divine struggle, or a boundless will set to dominate. It's only love—from the bottom to the top. God's love couldn't be contained. Nor could it be locked away in a warehouse. It spilled over into galaxies with stars and planets because God is God. And it keeps overflowing because no one's quite figured out how to make it stop. Creation has never stopped.

We are, each of us, God's love enfleshed and put in motion. It took four and a half billion years, but it finally spilled into you, Eden.

After Eden drew the pictures of the stars, I told her she wasn't with them. I told her something like this: God was making you, but it takes a long time to make babies. Memaw and Poppa had to love me and raise me. I had to grow up and go to school to meet Mommy. Then, we could have you. But we were thinking about you the whole time. You were in our dreams. In our prayers. We thought about what you would look like, how you would talk, and how you would grow. Now, you're finally with us. God made you at the perfect time—*kairos*.

And she replied, "Daddy, that's ridiculous."

The first thing we can say about ourselves is that we have been welcomed—unnecessarily so. God created room for something other than God to exist. How does anything come into being if God is all in all? God decided to withdraw into God and create a bench. Some Jewish kabbalistic thinkers call this *zimzum* (*tzimtzum* / *tsimtsum*), which is just as fun in pronunciation as theory. God must *zim* so we can *zum* (or something like that). There is no space for anything to exist until God contracts like a womb and pushes out a universe that will be a home for all living things.[2]

Creation, then, is the primal expression of hospitality, which might be defined as God's generous reception of all that is not God. There was no good reason to do this—God wasn't bored or lonely; God wasn't in the midst of an existential crisis, trying to find a new purpose with a new responsibility. And God knew there was a good chance the new guests would try to hijack the house by drinking, fighting, and spilling oil all over the rug. Yet, God took the risk and created. That's God's nature. Meister Eckhart says when the Trinity laughed together, they gave birth to us.[3] We are birthed out of nothing except God's joy.

God's very nature is the communion of hospitality. At the beginning of the story of God and humanity, God says, "Let us make humans in our image, according to our likeness" (Gen. 1:26). Wait, us? Who is us? Christians suggest it might be the Trinity: Father, Son, Spirit. Maybe that's right. The three-in-one God has perfectly mastered the art of hospitality, that God is wholly welcomed into God without overshadowing the individuality of God. God's being is communion, but there is still completeness in being apart from one another—a God who can be alone without ever being alone.

Your entire being is conditioned on welcoming and being welcomed; nothing lives without hospitality. Our planet is a perfect nursery for existence. Gather carbon, gravitational force, oxygen, and water in the perfect ratio, and a planet will welcome life. But if any of those dials were turned a millimeter in the wrong direction, the house would be harsh and unwelcoming to all life. You have been planted in the perfect garden for existence. It's Eden—a garden of delight.

Whenever we create space for another, we express the same profligate love inherent in God's nature—the One who welcomes us without necessity. All of this is a long-winded way of saying *Welcome*.

You belong here.

God has made space for you.

Embraced by Family and Friends

Robert Frost says, "Home is the place where, when you have to go there, they have to take you in."[1] We receive our earliest welcome and instruction in the basics of hospitality from our families.

My first real memory of being welcomed occurred when my younger sister was born and I was moved into my older brother's room. This was a relief. I had recently seen a snippet of a vampire movie by accident and had been sleeping with my fingers clenched around my neck for a month. I welcomed the extra company. Sometimes, I woke up in the middle of the night with a strange tickle under my rib cage. I lunged quickly to my brother's bed for safekeeping. Don't get me wrong: I wasn't under the illusion that he could kill a vampire with his bare hands, but I knew there was a fifty-fifty chance that the undead would grab him while I escaped.

Thank God.

The first thing my older brother did was take a piece of masking tape and run it down the middle of the room. "Build the wall," he chanted. Isn't this natural? The stranger is almost always a threat before a gift. *What's the cost?* we ask. To my place, my stuff, my privacy? I was quarantined to my side of the room, unwelcome in the space of another. It didn't last long—maybe just a week—because he realized he needed someone to beat in make-believe He-Man battles. A roommate was a small price to pay for the glory of victory.

Even at a young age, we experiment with boundaries—hosts and guests, inclusion and exclusion. Sometimes, we build a wall to keep someone out but realize we've imprisoned ourselves. Life is richer when it's shared.

Today, I watch my children make room for one another when monsters lurk under their beds or they keep thinking about the wet bandits from *Home Alone*. No one charges rent. Everyone sleeps better. Eventually, everyone garners enough strength to climb into their beds, and we will all synchronously mutter, "Thank you, my precious Lord." In the meantime, we are learning that we need people who will open their hearts, make a bed, and tuck you in.

One's welcome into family is their first and most crucial welcome. Each of us is welcomed into another's body. When a parasite enters an egg, we witness the miracle, sacrifice, and threat of hospitality. Right away, mothers realize that welcoming another person is always inconvenient and they'll never sleep. The bundle of cells swimming in amniotic fluid will stay too long or not long enough. It will bestow unfathomable moments of joy, or it will make you barf. It can even get you killed.

I've been lucky to have a family that has made a space for me during every step of my journey: in a body, a house, a calendar, a bank account, and a Netflix subscription. My parents have given themselves ceaselessly for my siblings and me.

Henri Nouwen says children are our most important guests; they stay for only a short period before they leave to chart their own paths.[2] That's why Erich Fromm describes parenthood as a long process of letting go. A child starts beside a mother's heart, grows to the size of a pumpkin, and takes up the mother's whole body. The child is born outside her body, and then he feeds from her chest. But from that moment on, the child moves further and further away—he crawls and then walks on his own, toddles, goes to school, maybe plays sports, chases girls. Then, the child leaves home. He begins to make his own decisions—good and bad. Each step is a distance away from Mom and Dad. Along the way, the parents are stricken with pride or relief, guilt and anger, and too much sadness. Many moms wish they could keep them safe forever, as in the womb. Dads want to help their kids back on the bike—over and over again. But they can't. Eventually, parents must let go. Their arms stretch only so far, and they can only carry their children so far and for so long.

Children, after all, never belong to anyone but God. We think we have power over these small people because they share our eyes and facial structure or our rhythm of speech. We do not. Your child is always a stranger, a mystery, a guest who needs the attention, boundaries, and care to grow into personhood. The task of parenting is to create a space for the child to listen to their inner life, receive experiences, and develop the courage to become their true selves. Welcome them as such, and they'll grow and thrive.

Families, in this sense, are our first training in the reception of the other. In our families, we receive the opportunity to open our lives, tables, and beds to the very people who know us better than ourselves. We encounter another being as a complete person rather than someone we can use, control, or create into an image of ourselves—at least, that's how it's supposed to go. These people are not the best supporting actors in your Oscar-nominated screenplay. If you can begin to welcome a spouse or kids (or a dog that can't get control of his bladder), you might eventually learn to welcome those who don't share your last name.

The problem is that not everyone has a family member to turn to when the monsters under the bed appear. It's tough when your family members are the monsters. Psychologists and counselors know the horrors of children who have not been properly welcomed. Fathers are absent for weeks at a time, while mothers have faulty expectations of their children. And vice versa. Houses are split down the middle, and children are asked to choose a side. We fail our children when our expectations of them are too high or too low—when we're too selfish. Too often, we ask them to rescue us from our boring or empty lives, but our existential fulfillment is a heavy burden for a child to bear. The trauma can last a lifetime: attachment issues, anxiety, and codependency. Families are excellent job security for psychologists, counselors, and social workers.

The Bible often seems foreign or otherworldly (because it is), but its description of families has remained oddly relevant. That's because most biblical families are more depraved than our own. It would be a stretch to feature a biblical family in James Dobson's *Focus on the Family*. Look at the very first family: Adam and Eve, the parents of Cain and Abel. It's not long until one brother doesn't get his due and permanently severs the family by murdering his brother. It's accurate. Imagine how Prince William would feel if they threw Harry on the throne. Cain and Abel are incarnate in every argument about familial inheritance. Jealousy runs deep.

When I read the story of Esau and Jacob as a child, I was envious of Jacob's ingenuity in duping his older brother, Esau. In the story, Isaac, the father, wants to bless Esau, whom he loves (biblical parents do have favorite children, by the way). His wife, Rebecca, loves the other son, Jacob. Rebecca takes advantage of her husband's blindness and comes up with this scheme to have Isaac bless the wrong kid. Jacob throws goatskin on his arms to simulate Esau's woolly body, and his blind father gives him everything. Jacob escapes with the inheritance, but he is estranged for years.

The same pattern continues—ad infinitum.

Many biblical stories are prescriptive, offering sage advice on living, goodness, and morality. Others are revelatory, revealing the reality of the human condition. In the Bible, families aren't often prescriptive, offering portraits of exemplary living. Instead, they show the depravity of the human condition under the worst systems of oppression. Men take multiple women as partners and wives, favoring one woman and shattering the others. Mothers try to strike deals with God to have children. Sometimes it works. When it doesn't, her husband is free to find a child elsewhere. Children eschew their parents' expectations and rebel against them while their parents mourn their deaths. No matter how many sermon series you hear on "biblical parenting," they will always exclude Abraham's hike up Mount Moriah, where he puts a knife to his son's throat.

Here's the point: It's biblically normal to have racist, misogynist family members who drink too much, battle demons, or are emotionally immature. You don't want a biblical family—I promise. This, of course, is one reason why God is intent on creating a bigger family.

The Hebrew practice of hospitality, *hachnasat orchim* (the welcoming of the guests), is founded on the belief that the tribes we create are always too small. More room is possible. And necessary. It's ingrained in the wastefulness of the Creator, who welcomes us without necessity. Who in their right mind would believe that? A people who know what it's like to be welcomed. The entire Hebrew Bible is thick with hospitality: Abram left home at the ripe age of seventy-five, dependent on God and others, as he walked toward the promised land; Jethro welcomed Moses when he escaped from Egypt; Ruth shared a deep connection to her mother-in-law, Naomi. Hospitality is ingrained in the muscle memory of the Jewish people because there is no life apart from welcoming and being welcomed.

Welcome the stranger because you know what it's like to be one (Lev. 19:34). The Israelites were enslaved in Egypt, a narrow place (*mitzrayim*), where Pharaoh constricted their lives, work, and wombs. Freedom was only possible when the Israelites unfurled their fingers and grabbed God's hand as God led them into the promised land. The people of God opened their hands and have kept them open ever since—well, mostly. Sustenance flows freely to and from their lives as they open their homes to the widows and orphans and let the poor and the immigrants glean from their fields. When you know you are created, you also know the world does not belong to you—it's God's. In God's world, there is always room to share.

Another reason you ought to welcome the stranger is because strangers wear the face of God. When three strangers show up at Abraham's doorstep looking for rest and refuge, his response is the most unnatural of the available options. This is to say that he doesn't hide behind the couch like the rest of us. Miracle of miracles, he invites them inside without thinking twice about his decision. Abraham bows at the feet of these strangers and gets to work gathering water. His wife, Sarah, begins to mix the finest flour with the yeast. His servants butcher the calf, and the table is set. These three visitors announce that Abraham and Sarah will bear a child. Enemies don't often feel like enemies after roasted lamb and wine.

And that's why it's always a good idea to set an extra plate at the table. The best gifts come from the hands of strangers, the people who offer no RSVP and have terrible manners. A guest might be an angel, a messenger from God, or even God incarnate (disguised as the person you least want to encounter). God, or one of God's minions, has a propensity to just show up in rags or as a solicitor trying to sell something. They might even offer to save your soul. Strangers are sometimes a nuisance. Other times, they are divine. Almost always, they are both. Esther de Waal, in her work on Benedictine spirituality, suggests that at the end of our hospitable activity, we are faced with two questions: "Did we see Christ in them? Did they see Christ in us?"[3]

This became clear in Jesus, the most Other, the One with an infinite qualitative distinction from humanity.[4] God broadened and deepened the smallest institution available—the marriage of Abram and Sarai—until the broken branch sprouted the most beautiful flower of them all: Jesus. Jesus is God's indiscriminate and extravagant hospitality enfleshed. Jesus's own ontology, his very own being, created space, crossed boundaries, and welcomed the other. In Mary's pregnant body, God is welcomed into humanity. In her fetus, God welcomes humanity into the divine. The body of Jesus tore down the dividing wall between God and humans and grafted all into the Tree of Life.

Humans aren't naturally inclined toward hospitality to the stranger. Almost immediately, it was evident that God was not welcome here. The Christ child was turned away at the first Christian worship service because there was no room in the inn. With no house of his own, Jesus made the whole world into an inn by welcoming people to mountainsides, dinner tables, gardens, and parties—these are the common spaces that belong to him because they belong to all. Jesus's ministry begins with strangers, under the stars, or in a musty basement that reeks of cigarette smoke. He finds his deepest belonging in the gutter with the kinds of people born in a barn—the ones who don't have their lives together, have lost their reason for living, or can't stop mourning the death of possibility.

These are the strangers that find their home in one another.

One of the most unbelievable parts of Jesus's life was that he never married or had children. This was unthinkable for a person from a tradition that commands him to go forth and multiply. How could this be? I like to think Jesus never had biological children because he was too busy creating a family with room for every widow, orphan, and stray who didn't know where to find their next meal. Jesus says, "My family—my real family—is anyone who does my will" (see Matt. 12:48–50). If you need a family, then you're in luck.

Here's your new mother and father: God.

And your brothers and sisters? In Jesus, they're from every nation and tribe.

Hospitality, then, became the defining characteristic of the early church. The first church wrestled with its heritage of inclusion as a band of messianic Jews tried to make sense of their Levitical and purity codes in light of Christ. What do we do with these people who won't get circumcised? The Spirit of Pentecost blew these strangers into their houses and lives. People, who were often unpleasant or unwanted, discovered a group of Jesus-followers who would pay attention to them, look them in the eye, and liberate them from their narrow lives. With little tongues of fire hovering over their heads, these strangers were comprehended, not just heard. They each found someone willing to learn their language. With the broken bread, they broke their lives wide open.

Rosaria Butterfield says hospitality turns strangers into neighbors and neighbors into family.[5] The ties of kinship and blood were just as strong in the culture in which Jesus lived and ministered. But Jesus challenged his first followers—and us, still today—to think about our families as open, not closed, units. The church, at least on paper, is a family that has nothing to do with blood or DNA. It's the name we use to describe the relationships that exist through space and time in the Holy Spirit. We could all use more family: additional children, bonus parents, new aunts and uncles.

It turns out that these people are all around us, free for the taking. They'll open their doors, and you're free to walk in.

Friendship is one of the ways we name those people in our bonus families. One of life's most incredible plot twists is waking up and realizing that friendship is hard. It's incongruous. Nothing previously has suggested that I might sit on the couch alone with no time or energy to go out for a drink, even as an introvert.

ANCIENT EXTRAVAGANCE

Our lack of belonging, especially as youth and adults, is a cultural epidemic. Aristotle thought friendship should be the primary human institution and that the overall health of a society could be measured by its conditions to sustain friendships. Considering our society's addiction to fast food, technology, and long work hours—we may be on life-support. Most Americans suffer from what Mother Teresa called the leprosy of the West. We've closed ourselves in, becoming an inhospitable place for the world. In the American economy, salvation is having enough money to pay for help. Sanctification, complete holiness, is self-reliance. Most of us are lonely, but at least we're self-sufficient.

The modern problem is that we work ourselves to death to save ourselves from the one thing that actually will save us: friendships.[6]

Childhood was the golden age of friendships for me. They were easy and plentiful—full of afternoons in the woods, swing sets, and gangs of bicycles patrolling the streets. My adolescent years were invested around cars in the high school parking lot, church vans, or on open fields with soccer balls and frisbees. All of this escalated until I went to college and lived in a two-hundred-and-fifty-square-foot box with another person. Friendship was arguably the most efficient college curriculum for self-discovery and maturity. I met the very people who posed life's most difficult questions over burnt coffee and greasy hash browns; they even walked with me until I discovered the answers (which are usually more difficult questions).

Friendships were not a part of my life but life itself.

Then, you enter your thirties. Worse: the forties, the decade when little gray hairs sprout on your face like strands of dying grass. Every encroaching decade threatens you with debilitating isolation. Friendship requires space for another to take up residence in your life, and that space has already been filled with other competing goods—usually kids and sleep. Or, sleep because of kids. My priorities have changed. For instance, playgrounds have become cool again. The workforce is also a culprit. Friendships are terribly inefficient because they require time around kitchen tables, and time is in short supply. Life is complicated and busy enough without another person's issues.

As we age, most of our relationships are acquaintances. You know, the coworkers who are fun around the office but will thankfully disappear when you take a new job. There's the person who will meet you at the playground (remember, they're cool again) to complain about children. Others might even be interested in hoppy beer or esoteric theology written by dead Europeans. Thanks to our digital immersion into social media, "friends" are casually procured by clicking an icon on a screen. These people are great to have around, if only as a form of capital—a service for utility and pleasure, or what Aristotle calls imperfect friendships. But few of them will come to love our peculiarities or care to learn what keeps us up at night (their names are Pax and Eden).

And yet, we also need people to share more than parenting hacks, our lament over politics, and an affinity for Duke basketball. What about the friends who are comfortable enough to share (mostly) everything, including being together in silence? As Augustine says, these are the few people who are sweet beyond the sweetness of life.[7]

Friendship is about the hospitality of the heart. In friends, we learn to invite people into our hearts, which are our deepest, most intimate homes. Friends are inside jokes and trips down memory lane; mom's spaghetti and dad's pork chops manifest in a person. Comfort incarnate. They draw you out of yourself, enlarging your world by opening you up, listening to you, and affirming you. You become better than you ever could be on your own. Augustine talked about one of his friends as the other half of his soul.[8] Think of the heart necklaces that elementary-aged girls buy at Claire's and share with their best friends. One half says "best," and the other half says "friend." Children know what we forget: Your heart is only whole when shared.

I've discovered that we've got our priorities all backward or that we've forgotten what we learned so early on in life—there is no growth apart from another human being. Friendship is more than an escape from life; it's the very substance of living well. To be even more precise, friendship is the point of living; nothing is more important. Aristotle also wrote, "Without friends, no one would want to live, even if he had all other goods."[9]

It takes work. But it's good work, because the promise of the American dream of success and self-sufficiency is accompanied by twin vices: loneliness and emptiness.

Aristotle also believed that friendship was a virtue, or at the least, requires virtues to be sustained. I think he's right—friendships don't spontaneously mature without proper care. It takes forgiveness to see past another's posturing, masquerading, and inability to return text messages. Or, how about the patience it takes to send another text message anyway? There's the benevolence to drop off a care package of soup when one can't get off the couch. Endurance will reignite a lapsed relationship after years of dormancy. Hospitality can open the doors of your heart for a stranger to step inside, regardless of risk and mistrust. How about the sacrifice to see another person's well-being as your most important priority?

Friendship, then, is the best pattern for becoming a Christian—to love and be loved by God and one another. The reverse must also be true: Christianity bestows the virtues necessary to sustain a friendship. After all, what is Christianity except becoming a friend of the world?

Scripture could be read as the story of God's befriending of the world. This is why God created the world in the first place—that we might have space to be and to receive the gift of the other. Karl Barth said, "[God] does not will to be God without us, and He does not will that we should be without Him. . . . God does not exist in solitude but in fellowship."[10] Thus, God undertook incarnation in Jesus for one reason: friendship.

Someone once said Jesus's best miracle was having twelve close friends after the age of thirty. These disciples become his best friends, the other half of his heart: "I do not call you servants any longer, because a servant does not know what the master is doing, but I have called you friends" (John 15:15). It was a surprising move. God could have left them aloof as servants or subordinate children but instead invited them into all the love and pain in his heart. It was a terrible deal. The cost-to-benefit ratio was lousy. They couldn't reciprocate the gesture; all they could offer was death.

True friendship, by its nature, is inherently risky. That's because it's the most profound form of hospitality. Etymologically, "hostility" is located within the word *hospitality*. Risk is built into the very fabric of hospitality, because hospitality contains its opposite within it. Hospitality comes from the Latin *hospes*, built upon two words: *hostis*, which originally meant "stranger or enemy," and *pets*, which means "to have power." In every welcome, there is a power struggle. This is why French deconstruction philosopher Jacques Derrida created a neologism, "hostipitality," to indicate the potential of hostility within hospitality.[11]

To welcome, or be welcomed, is always to receive the chance of being hurt. Every time we love, we open ourselves up to potential pain. C. S. Lewis says, "To love at all is to be vulnerable. Love anything, and your heart will certainly be wrung and possibly be broken. If you want to make sure of keeping it intact, you must give your heart to no one, not even to an animal."[12] Once inside your house, someone can break your lamp or steal your cash from the dresser. They can open the packaged toy from the nineties that you've had stashed away for years. God forbid—they might even drink your last Diet Dr Pepper. But if you think inviting someone into a house is hard, try asking them into your life. Your heart is more fragile than plates and glasses. A broken heart is not easily repaired.

In John's account of the Last Supper, Jesus describes the depth of his understanding of friendship: To live as a friend is to demonstrate the highest form of love, which is the willingness to die for one another. Jesus embodies sacrifice to challenge the purely economic character of our relationships that sees people only for their usefulness or future benefit. Every one of Jesus's friends betrays, denies, and abandons him. Jesus never gave up on them. He meets Peter, who denied him three times, around a campfire and offers forgiveness. He does this for all of us—even Judas. No place is safe from Jesus's friendship, not even hell itself.

In *The Fellowship of the Ring* by J. R. R. Tolkien, Frodo, the hobbit, arrives at Crickhollow and is determined to destroy the ring alone without exposing his friends to the danger that will lie ahead. He tries to break off when Merry, Pippin, and Sam confront him before he can slip away:

> "It all depends on what you want," put in Merry. "You can trust us to stick to you through thick and thin—to the bitter end. And you can trust us to keep any secret of yours—closer than you keep it yourself. But you cannot trust us to let you face trouble alone and

go off without a word. We are your friends, Frodo.... We are horribly afraid—but we are coming with you; or following you like hounds."[13]

Friendship was an essential weapon against the evil in Middle Earth. That's true on our earth, too, today and always. The risk and cost of friendship is greater than the alternative life of isolation and loneliness. To know and be known by another, regardless of the risk, is the only way to live genuinely.

Friendship may be a virtue essential for a culture that's ripe with depression, partisanship, and busyness. The world is crushingly lonely for more people than we know. You might think you can get along just fine without others, but I have never been the kind of person who can survive with just a clingy cat and a good book. Don't get me wrong. I like cats and books as much as the next introvert, but I also know that the most meaningful parts of my life happen around a table, when my kids sit in another person's lap, and the rest of us open ourselves to see and be seen.

Here's the point: You really ought to try to respond to that text message. Keep the weekly check-in, the monthly dinner, the yearly retreat. You might have nerves and butterflies and a deep dread about another evening activity, but I am here to remind you that time with friends will almost always make you feel better—more alive, more loving, more yourself. I guess I've learned that friendship is a spiritual discipline, or a means to abide in God by abiding in another. Friendship is a practice; like all other practices, it takes work.

* * *

Friendship is wasteful, like all the other best parts of our lives. C. S. Lewis continues: "Friendship is unnecessary, like philosophy, like art, like the universe itself.... It has no survival value; rather, it is one of those things which give value to survival."[14]

Lewis isn't completely correct. Hospitality, as we've seen, *is* a matter of life and death. Nothing lives without it. And that's why the church is such good news: We are the people who have to take you in whether we want to or not.

At Home in Body and Spirit

It's said that the Jewish people put doors on all four sides of their houses so a stranger could find welcome from any direction. That's a bit overboard if you ask me. It's another one of those strange customs that make no sense in our culture. Most Americans give the universal sign that you are not welcome by shutting the garage door promptly at five p.m. Earlier if possible. Please don't interrupt us. Visitors are welcome, but they'll have better luck finding recourse if they RSVP. Like every other millennial, I expect a phone call before a knock on the door. A text message before a phone call is appreciated, too.

Many of the biblical stories of hospitality bring about a surge of anxiety. In one story, Jesus stopped by the house of two sisters, Mary and Martha, completely unannounced. If you like Jesus but don't like interruptions, then you're in trouble. This particular visit must have occurred near mealtime, because Martha went straight into the kitchen with one thing on her mind: hospitality, the hallmark of the Jewish home. She gathered, prepared, cooked, and set. No time to waste in holy leisure when work is to be done.

Meanwhile, Martha's sister, Mary, sat in the common room conversing with Jesus. Can't you imagine her giggling at Jesus's feet while Martha is ready to murder her for not putting down the wine glass and helping with the preparations? There is no communal meal without the meal. Martha cried out: "Lord, do you not care that my sister has left me to do all the work by myself? Tell her, then, to help me" (Luke 10:40).

If you've ever hosted a dinner party, you can likely relate to Martha. It's hard to invite people into your home. It's usually too messy or too small. In our case, it's too small *and* too messy. The kids' toys are scattered across the floor or pet smells linger in the air. Sometimes both. If you have low ceilings, you must worry about tall people. If you have small tables, then you have to worry about seating. Dirty clothes are spilling out of the laundry hamper. The toilet hasn't flushed right for an entire year. You must be sure to warn the visitors about the clingy dog that will shove her nose right in their crotch. Someone always needs to run to the corner store and grab a bottle of wine. Should I vacuum, you wonder? I should probably vacuum.

The annoying part of the story is that Martha must be thinking through every conceivable detail of hospitality while Jesus praises Mary, who simply sits and listens. "Martha, Martha," Jesus said, "you are worried and distracted by many things, but few things are needed—indeed, only one. Mary has chosen the better part" (Luke 10:41–42).

Until recently, I didn't fully understand why Mary had made the better decision. My family hosted a small group in our house. In good Martha fashion, we prepared everything the best we could (that's to say, we cooked an edible meal and bought cheap wine—we never make promises about kid clutter). The meal was progressing just wonderfully until someone had the nerve to ask the group, "What's a recent experience that gave you hope?"

The easy answer was the Atlanta Braves, who were on a ten-game winning streak. The honest answer was that I felt rather hopeless; my work was not stimulating, my kids were getting too much screen time, and the world was frowning. I needed a nap. I would much rather get back in the kitchen and refill glasses than answer that barbaric question. It's so much easier to let people into your house without actually letting them into your home.

That's when it struck me. The veil dropped. I realized why Jesus said Mary had chosen the better part. Friendship and conversation are bread, too—that which fills your soul with sustenance and life.

Martha opened her home to Jesus, but Mary opened her heart.

As it happens, Martha's actions were not criticized; hospitality is essential. The difference is that Jesus seems to care less about whether the space is tidy and more about the people gathered around the table. Appearances are always deceiving. Jesus knows you can paint a wall damaged by water, but that doesn't mean there's no mold growing on the other side. A whitewashed tomb is still full of rot and decay, he would later tell the Pharisees (Matt. 23:27). In other words, you can vacuum all the crumbs from the floor, set out the finest china, and cook a perfect piece of chicken, but it doesn't eradicate the hopelessness you feel in your heart. What's the use of entering one's home without being welcomed into their *real* life?

The first task of following Jesus is learning to properly and faithfully welcome him. Jesus doesn't keep us around so we can do things for him but so that we can abide with him. He's interested in friendship. Not service. Mary sat at her teacher's feet, willing to learn from him and become his student and disciple. Jesus entered not just her home but her heart.

Most churches I know resemble Martha rather than Mary. When I was first learning to be a pastor, our denomination's megachurch guru enlightened us with three easy steps to create a megachurch. (Later, I learned that there was a fourth, undisclosed step to Christian stardom: plant a church in the suburbs right before a housing boom.) One of the three steps I remember is that the service has to get on without a hitch. No one wants to attend a church where readers stumble over the words, the sermon was written on Saturday night, and the communion liturgy has had a typo for half a year. You must act like you're expecting visitors and handle the housekeeping accordingly. The church needs a "hospitality" committee with a strategic plan: name badges, reserved spaces for visitors, and directions to the bathroom. It's Disney World—but with Jesus. Say things like, "My pleasure!" "You belong here!" "Jesus loves you!"

Church is doing our best work and smiling too much.

There's certainly an argument to be made for doing our best work. I get it: No one has time for an improvised sermon on "the Good Samaritan" and a choral medley that wasn't rehearsed. "Verb Church" down the road has a full light show, coffee bar, and special appearance by a D-list celebrity.

Preparation matters. We offer God our best sacrifice of worship, just as the Israelites offered their choice lambs.

Many churches have gotten pretty good at welcoming physical bodies. There are ramps, signs, gluten-free communion, and rocking chairs for nursing mothers. In some churches, you can smell like Christian Dior, or you can smell like the streets. All of this is good and necessary.

Fewer churches are equipped to welcome the poor in spirit. You can limp in physically but not mentally or spiritually. Henri Nouwen writes that hospitality in our culture conjures images of "tea parties, bland conversation, and a general atmosphere of coziness."[1] I wonder if that's also true of churches. Here's the problem: Increasingly, the kinds of people who want to come to church post-Christendom will care less about performance and more about finding a space where they are seen—where they can explore their faith without fear of judgment, loneliness, and hopelessness.

One of my first regrets as a pastor took place as I was greeting parishioners as they entered the sanctuary. I was standing in the narthex when a woman flew through the doors. She often had problems; there was a lot of heartache. Once a month, she'd get drunk, call my landline, cuss me out, and profusely apologize the next morning. I stuck out my hand and said, "Good morning." Completely ignoring our shared cultural script, she replied, "Bad morning," and hurried to her car before I could apologize for speaking carelessly. She was looking for a place to bring her lament or something else, and there I was, standing in a suit and smiling way too much.

Most of us don't want to talk about our pain, but there's nowhere to go when we find the courage. It's not hospitality if you must leave your humanity in the car as you walk to the doors. Like Frederick Buechner, I sometimes wonder if the best thing that could happen to a church is to lose its building and money; then all the people would have left is God and each other.

A friend recently told me he doesn't attend church because everyone fits in and no one belongs. Church is where you shift and adapt to meet the expectations of the gathered people. Men talk about college football because men are scripted to be tough and like sports. Women make compliments about shoes and skirts and hairstyles. The new mom cringes every time her newborn squeals. The toddler's father sits on the edge of his seat while she carries Christ's light into the sanctuary. There's a lot of pressure, especially for a six-year-old, to get the altar candles lit on the first dip (let alone not burn down the place). Church is a game of show and not tell—smile on the outside and cry on the inside. Everyone believes—no one questions. We are happy.

Conversely, belonging occurs when your whole self is welcomed regardless of what you wear outside or inside. You belong if you can't pray; you belong if you pray to "Daddy God." How do you know when you belong? Maybe it's when you don't have to continually explain why you are the way you are. It will feel like your identity (in all its strangeness) only increases your welcome, because they realize you are more mystery to explore and appreciate. They are comfortable telling you the truth. You know you're on the right track when they point out that your breath smells like a garbage can. You belong when you feel free to be an embodied, ensouled human being.

It sounds odd, but one of the reasons why my family started attending our current church is because it doesn't try to hide its imperfections. It's an anti-anxious church, more like Mary than Martha. It's completely satisfied to sit at Jesus's feet instead of hustling around the building to make sure all the preparations are in order. One recent Sunday, the person in front of me accidentally kicked over his wife's venti Starbucks coffee (an obnoxious name for an obnoxious amount of coffee). I immediately started praying for him. The coffee assailant quickly ran to get napkins while the twenty ounces of coffee ran from the pew to the stage. His spouse let him struggle in agony, knowing he brought napkins to a towel fight, before she eventually got up to help him. A good spouse, like God, is rarely early but never late.

If you walked into the sanctuary at the start of worship, you'd see an embarrassed man, four to five people on their hands and knees scrubbing the floor, and a pastor smiling and hugging his parishioners. Here's the message: Imperfect people are welcome here. That's the kind of anthropology or philosophy of the human condition that needs to be made clear at the start. God's house is where it's normal to admit we make a mess of things—we are a hospital for sinners and not a museum of the saints.

You're free to leave it on the altar, whether it's your cup of coffee or your entire heart.

Later in worship, our pastor serendipitously quoted an episode of *Friends* where Jennifer Aniston's character, Rachel, spilled spaghetti on Joey's floor. She profusely apologized, knowing how anal Monica was about cleanliness. But Joey quickly remarked, "You're at Joey's." He smiled and threw his own spaghetti on the floor.

"I've never lived like this before," said Rachel.

Joey's house has different rules.

We all need a place where we are free to be humans, to pour out our lives in a place that can hold the weight. God's dream for the church is to be a home for the homeless.

· · · · · · · · · · · · · · · · · ✦ · · · · · · · · · · · · · · · · ·

In the Gospel of John, Jesus is back in Bethany having dinner with his friends Mary and Martha.[2] Not long before, Jesus had pulled Lazarus out of the grave. He was a few days late to work but still got the job done. Now, Martha is behind the stove, finishing up dinner, setting the table, and pouring the stew in their bowls. Lazarus has his feet kicked up at the table. Mary is nowhere to be found. Typical. When dinner is finally ready, they take their seats, and Mary enters the dining room with a one-pound jar of 100 percent clean, unadulterated nard. It's a pound of perfume.

I've gotten in some pretty precarious situations with my wife, but I've never bought her more than three and a quarter ounces. Imagine entering the local Macy's and telling the salesperson, "Sure, that smells pretty nice. I think I'll have a pound, please."

Mary takes the nard, pops the top, and pours it all over Jesus's feet. The house fills up with the aroma—everyone's sneezing and coughing. Lazarus grabs palms to waft the scent out the doors while Mary kneels at Jesus's feet. She takes the clip out of her hair, lets her hair down, and starts mopping his feet with her hair. It's weird. It would've been weirder around AD 30. In this culture, women don't touch men's feet; it's risqué and disgraceful. Some say it would be like a woman touching a man's inner thigh.

Judas catches the whole scene out of the corner of his eye. He takes a look at the bottle and sees the label. It's Black Label Nard. The stuff is worth three hundred denarii. Now, one denarius was an average daily wage. To do a bit of translation, three hundred denarii is equivalent to pouring at least thirty thousand dollars of perfume on someone's feet. He watches the nard soak into Jesus's skin and clothes; some spills over into the dust and creates a dirt clod of potpourri.

Judas, flabbergasted by this sequence of events, shouts, "Why was this perfume not sold for three hundred denarii and the money given to the poor?" (John 12:5). The perfume could have fed a family for a year, made the down payment for a new community kitchen, or started a foundation for lepers. Better yet, if you gave the money to the Jewish temple, it could have been distributed evenly to those in real need. Like Martha, Judas asks Jesus, "Do you not care?" It's a bit like lighting cash on fire. Why the waste?

Jesus, the guy who spends all his free time at the brothels and the homeless shelters, tells Judas to "leave her alone."

The irony is that Mary was, technically, giving to the poor. She poured out her most prized possession on a homeless Jew. It was an act of worship. Later, Jesus would do the very same thing. In his death, his life would be poured out—every last drop—for the sake of the world. Mary reminds us—twice—that hospitality has nothing to do with custom and order. Enough with the disingenuous civility that distracts us from the one thing that truly matters: Jesus.

Wherever God is present, there must be wasteful extravagance. If you don't understand Mary's wastefulness, then you'll never understand the wastefulness of God. When people look at your life and church, do they see Mary or Martha? Is it calculated obedience or the reckless extravagance of hospitality? A Martha church knows how to receive someone's body, but a church that sits with Mary might learn to receive someone's soul.

If you've ever been in a polite church preoccupied with perfecting the whole performance, then you'll understand Mary. Take a bottle of perfume, or a venti coffee, or your life, and spill it all over the floor.

Church is where you bring your whole self and recklessly give it to God and one another.

After all, you're in God's house.

TWO

BEAUTY

Singing Is Who We Are

I remember what worship was like a long time ago, before its present marriage to entertainment. In the days before stage lighting, fog machines, and stadium seating with reclining chairs, worship was unremarkable. The congregations I attended flippantly breezed through theologically dense lyrics and obscure words. We raised our Ebenezers with no clue of what we raised. But the word sounded meaningful. And holy. As a child, I wanted it all to be over as soon as possible.

Then again, this is a matter of preference. God encounters us through cultural means. Plenty of worshippers find White European hymns about substitutionary atonement absolutely exhilarating. I'm not one of those people.

The hymns I sang growing up were accompanied by the piano or organ and conducted by a man who used a little too much vibrato. I didn't have a natural friendship with the organ—not at first. As a kid, I personified all the musical instruments with stereotypes of people: The electric guitar must be a twentysomething kid wearing black skinny jeans. The drum might be an African. The piano is, and always will be, my mother, who plays the piano sometimes but not nearly as often as she should. But the organ was an elderly British man with a handlebar mustache and a pipe dangling from his lip. The organ felt old but distinguished. He had been a family friend for over one thousand years who I knew I should respect and trust, but I wasn't sure how to talk with him for a long time.

And so, I spent most of my time coloring. As best as I can remember, churches did not create busy bags for kids. If your mother didn't bring crayons and paper, then your artistic medium would be golf pencil on bulletin paper—"Pastor Preaching Sermon," another portrait shoved in your mother's purse at the end of the service and thrown out later that week.

I counted things the rest of the time (as any child destined for therapy would). There were six squares on the pattern next to the cross, which created twenty-four corners. The decorative lights hanging from the ceiling also had six panels. If the light to my right suddenly fell from the ceiling, then it would've landed right on Mr. Thompson and his family. And the sanctuary had twelve pews on each side (is this intentional?), and each pew had about eight people, making ninety-six people on each side (I double-checked these statistics weekly to ensure nothing had changed). If nothing else, worship made me a better mathematician and jump-started an obsessive counting compulsion.

I must have asked my mom, "Why must we sing?"

The answer was, "That's who we are."

· ◆ ·

Beauty is not immediately categorized and explained in terms of its usefulness. So much about the arts feels wasteful in a world that worships efficiency. Ask an art major who threw away her life to play with clay and charcoal pencils. Every summer vacation, she is destined to return home to answer a whole series of questions from people who can't speak of value outside of reductive utilitarianism:

What is it you're doing?

Drawing?

Is that really education?

Did you take out loans for that?

Do you plan on living with your parents after graduation?

And so on.

My wife quilts blankets, which must be the most wasteful of all art forms. "Why make a quilt when one could buy a mass-manufactured blanket?" I ask my wife this as she spends hours locked in a closet that has become a sewing room.

Originally, quilting was almost entirely utilitarian, allowing early American settlers to use and reuse all their resources. Two worn-out blankets could be blended, combined with other leftover fabric to make a thicker comforter to throw on the bed or cover unsealed windows. All things made new.

Today, it's a different story. My wife endures the painstaking process of sitting down with fabric, scissors, and thread (even though she can grab a similar blanket for $25.99 at Target in Midtown). Maybe she knows that not all stitches are created equal. We are meant to be clothed in beauty.

There is an inherent purposelessness deep within beauty. And the arts help us resist the notion that everything in our world must be instrumentalized to some purpose. No one spends the first two hours of their day watching a sunrise because it's efficient. Meditating on Rembrandt's painting of the Prodigal Son for half an hour must not be biologically necessary. And Henri Nouwen's breathtaking book on the painting isn't likely to affect natural selection. All I know is that I feel more human after watching sunrises, spending time with Rembrandt, and reading Nouwen.

Maybe the real reason behind singing, creating, and dancing is that there is a thirst for beauty laden deep within each of us. Saint Basil the Great says humans desire the beautiful by nature. We long for something that transcends the finite.

The Creator made us to co-create. "Maybe the desire to make something beautiful is the piece of God that is inside each of us," says Mary Oliver.[1] In our creation, our lives are bound to a God who brings order to chaos, which means our lives are bound up in creating. When we encounter something captivating or enchanting, we are inspired to raise the bar and create something beautiful in our lives.

This is creativity: filtering matter, experiences, and information into something that makes us feel alive. In this case, beauty is thicker than just the arts—painting, sculpting, photographing. We rearrange our furniture and the apps on the home screen of our phones. We doodle during a boring meeting. We might create a thank-you note to a friend. We combine ingredients to create new flavors and textures that stun and tantalize the mouth.

It is the work of scientists, engineers, and anyone who dares to enter the process of making.

Under our creative care, life becomes more than the sum of its parts; instead, we are integrated into the transcendent world of the Creator.

We become the kinds of beings we were meant to become.

The arts, and music in particular, seem to be universal. Cultures have found ways to thrive without the written word, but music is always present in human civilization. Jeremy Begbie writes that music spans the entire range of humanity. "Even the most poverty-stricken peoples will sing," he says.[2] Humans stranded on a desert island would naturally first secure their food, but how long would it take to find instruments for music? The development of a community is also the creation of a particular song.

The Hebrew people thought music was necessary for existence—it was the auditory avenue to convey their stories, values, and beliefs. In Genesis, the ancestor of all those who play the lyre and the pipe is mentioned alongside the first smith and cattle breeder (see Genesis 4). This means the ancestor who taught them to make music is as essential as the ancestor who gave them the gift of beef and milk. Beauty is as necessary to human flourishing as eating.

Music was a part of the daily lives of the Israelites, accompanying almost every facet of the human experience: working, celebrating, resting, fighting, lamenting, and sleeping. Much of life and love and God can't be explained, so it must be sung. Doesn't music expose the limits of our language? Your first kiss, for instance, can't be rationally explained. How do you put your last kiss, then, into words? Words and images can help explain something, but they always fall short in their descriptive prowess. If it's a part of existence, then there is an accompanying song. And those songs have been collected and compiled in a book called the Psalms.

Psalms is the hymnal of 150 songs placed right in the middle of the Christian Bible. It is the heart, in location and purpose, that pumps blood throughout the rest of the narrative. For thousands of years, the

Judeo-Christian tradition has relied on Psalms as a guide through the changing of times. They are our school for prayer and catechesis in learning to talk to God. Or maybe they're also a type of clothing for our inner life.

Life, says Walter Brueggemann, moves from orientation into disorientation and then back into reorientation.[3] And that's the cycle of our days and years. There are longer days and shorter nights, as there is joy and lament. There is cold and warmth, as there is anger and thanksgiving. There is freezing rain and cursing. We teach our bodies how to cope with new seasons at a very young age. There's clothing appropriate to the weather like plaid and winter coats or miniskirts and swimming suits. But what about our inner life? What shall we wear when summer fades into fall and then drops deeper into winter?

We clothe ourselves in song.

The Psalms form our spiritual lives and permit us to bring our feelings to God no matter what joy or rage lingers in our hearts. What do you say when you hold a newborn baby? How about this: "You knit us together in our mothers' wombs. I praise you because we are fearfully and wonderfully made" (Ps. 139:13–14). Regrets take shape, and cursing is given permission. Say your worst; God has already heard it, and the church has canonized it. With confessional Psalms, our hearts are aired out like an open house.

The Psalms remind us that the most beautiful poems and songs arise out of the darkest circumstances. The songs of lament occur most frequently in the psalter, comprising about 40 percent of the hymnal. On my good days, that strikes me as the proper ratio. Maybe our lives aren't comprised of 40 percent sadness, but most of us could use the extra words when we can only speak through our tears.

Perhaps this is why families often request Psalms to be read at funerals. Poems set to music will always heal in a way that theology lectures can't. The raw emotion counteracts the platitudes about Grandma singing with a choir of angels and Daddy playing golf with Moses. In the mountains where I have lived, I have commonly read: "I lift up my eyes to the hills— from where will my help come? My help comes from the Lord, who made heaven and earth" (Ps. 121:1–2). Imagine reading that in a cemetery settled in the middle of a valley of dry bones, overwhelmed by the claustrophobia of death. It's a desperate plea for healing to the One who promises it.

Pain is a deep well. The most decadent ingredients for creativity will often come when you feel the world most intensely. When the Israelites dipped the bucket into the well, they drew out enough water to sustain us for millennia. Still today, their music speaks when our words fail.

A Lutheran theologian, Martin Marty, read through the Psalms with his wife during her struggle with cancer. The Psalms became their respite every night when she woke up to take her nausea medicine and waited to fall back asleep. One night, Martin's wife caught him skipping from Psalm 87 to 91. Some have called Psalm 88 the one with no hope; it's the one where the author writes, "Darkness is my only companion."

"Why did you skip that psalm?" his wife demanded.

Marty told her he wasn't sure she could take Psalm 88 that night.

"Please read it, for me," she said. "I need that kind the most."

The beauty of the Psalms is that most of them end in praise. Even the gravest laments and raging curses bend back to God's goodness and faithfulness. And that's the promise of the Psalms and the pattern for our lives. We will move from dark into light if the Psalms are any consolation. In fact, hope is just one chapter away—or maybe just a stanza. Life will be redeemed, and though it will never look and feel the same as a previous season, there is still the promise of reorientation.

Or maybe it's better to put it this way: There's always hope for a final season. And that's the season of resurrection.

· · · · · · · · · · · · · · · · · ✦ · · · · · · · · · · · · · · · · ·

Kathleen Norris says we go to church to sing, and theology is secondary.[4] God fills our words with his presence, and what cannot be contained overflows into our song. God is greater than what can be conceived—a mystery to be savored, not a question that can be answered. God can't be restrained by our words. In fact, whenever we say "God," we've already misspoken. How do we savor a mystery but through music?

After all, the doctrine of the Trinity makes no rational sense. I've yet to hear anyone draw it with a diagram or explain it with rational dogmatic statements. But I have experienced it through a three-note chord. Each note dwells with the other, creating room to enhance the life of the others.

We feel the Trinity, even if we can't understand the Trinity, and we become like God.

The Israelites have taught us that the God who exceeds all that can be fathomed and comprehended must be expressed with notes, harmony, and dissonance. There are deeper realities than what can be perceived with your brain. It's okay to feel something or receive a surge of unexpected delight. Dare I say that it's good? A song dresses the church's theology and doctrine in flowing gowns or tailored suits; the Easter hymns clothe the resurrection stories with golden crowns. The agony of the crucifixion is dressed in mourning. God transforms tears of sadness into tears of beauty. We don't just learn about the gospel; we feel it and embody it with our hearts and hands (that sometimes clap—off beat).

There might be easier ways to get the point across or to capture the image, but the song resists efficiency with rhythm and melody (this is true even when the tempo in "We Three Kings" is so slow that it takes an entire voyage to Bethlehem to finish the song). A people that sings knows that the world is ordered and full of surprise. The notes of rest are pregnant pauses where we know that the song will continue, even when it seems like nothing is happening. We are a people who expect tension and lament, but we also know to wait patiently. God can resolve it with praise. God will finish the song we started, weaving our missed notes into something we could never create on our own.

A friend told me she started crying uncontrollably when a hymn popped up on her Spotify playlist. She hadn't been to church in a couple of years. The hymn reminded her that a part of her was dying, and she might never get that piece back. She's unsure if she misses God but knows that she misses God's songs.

When we forget our songs, do we forget who we are?

There's something cathartic about being placed in a long tradition that knows it's okay to praise God and curse God. Speak the same healing words as those who have gone before us and those to come long after we're gone. They first belonged to David or Solomon and the postexilic community who wrote them out of their heartache and struggle. These are the songs Jesus prayed—the ones he may have memorized in Sabbath School and heard while he was tucked in at night by Mary and Joseph. Later, they became the words he quoted while hanging on the cross as death stole his voice.

Recently, I visited my grandmother, who is ninety-one years old, in a memory care facility. What do you say to someone who misses every question on the amnesia tests from the movies? She doesn't know her family, the president, or the day of the week. My mom, who visits her almost daily, reminded me she still knows how to sing. She may not know my name, but she remembers "Great Is Thy Faithfulness."

The song unlocks a deeper reality that's otherwise smothered by confusion. Immediately, a smile forms on her face, and she begins to relax. Her body begins to move and sway a little. And her lips open to form the same words she'd long forgotten. God calls out to her through the country twang of Alan Jackson.

> Thou changest not, thy compassions, they fail not;
> as thou hast been, thou forever wilt be.

She communicates with songs when she can't use her words. And the strum of the guitar allows her to experience a love that she can't remember how to put into words.

The songs of God and the church reunite her with her story—to the past she cannot remember and the future that has not been revealed. We glimpse her eternal future where she is not Alzheimer's—or old—or crazy. She puts on her name tag that reads *June Llewellyn: child of God*. When you're sitting in a memory care unit, what will people sing to you?

· · · · · · · · · · · · · · · ✦ · · · · · · · · · · · · · · ·

I'm glad I learned to suffer through the music and poems that others found beautiful but I didn't. Every Sunday, the songs remind me who I am. That's not to say I have come to like every song or agree with all the lyrics (I tend to sit out the ones that mention "blood," "debt," and "wrath"). There is a message in the sound of the music, just as there is a message in the lyrics. And I have learned to embody the music, even when I disagree with the lyrics.

More so, the music reminds me that I belong to the kind of people who sing. Outside of concerts and occasional sporting events, where else do we waste time singing together? We are a people of David, Charles Wesley, Bach, the great spirituals, and (unfortunately) Hillsong United. My personhood is found in a deep harmony that manifests and constitutes the people of God.

It rarely accomplishes much. Yet, it's the soundtrack to my life.

Cross-Shaped Pictures

I started taking photographs during the pandemic summer of COVID-19. To be clear, this was the first summer of COVID as opposed to all the low-budget sequels that have followed. My lockdown experience was happily dull. It took place in a rural mountain town, which meant I spent my time in the areas where the virus had no business being—winding trails and flowing rivers.

Time during the pandemic was formless. Clocks didn't matter, because I had nowhere to be. My biggest challenge was assuaging my compulsion to work. I am, by nature, anxious and prone to perfectionism. I needed to work but had no real work to accomplish. Most hours of the day, I wasn't working, but I wasn't not working either. It's fair to say that I was on call, but I was never called. The only time stamp was the obligatory Zoom call where all the unessential employees manufactured essential accomplishments.

I'm not a photographer, but I started taking pictures. I did this, as best as I can tell, to grasp the time—at least a part of it. Maybe I wanted to create a keepsake and capture time in a 4x6 rectangle or a few hundred pixels. That pandemic existed. I have a scrapbook of evidence.

Or did I start making pictures?

Does one take or make pictures? Maybe pictures are made as much as they are taken; they are created. Photographers pay attention to things like composition and lighting and mood and create their own representation of reality. We impress ourselves upon the object of our perception. There is no objective way of looking at a flower, for instance. You decide to look at it a certain way, from a certain angle, and create a representation of life. Some days, you capture the whole field. On other days, it's interesting enough to look at one petal. Each snap tells a story.

Photographers can bend moments and subjects to create the stories they want to tell. There is no one narrative that must be told—at any moment, numerous stories are available to be expressed. Take the classic snapshot of the coffee cup, Bible open, with the gingham Instagram filter. No one has to know that a toddler is screaming about hot chocolate one seat over. The moment is tranquil, despite the bratty toddler, because the first sip of your Americano brought peace to your soul.

You also have a brand to maintain.

My favorite image of the pandemic is a picture of my daughter in her swimming suit. She's sitting on an old, broken metal bench. She is wet from the Slip 'N Slide. She is pouting, with her head resting on one of her palms. The harsh afternoon light washes out the vibrant colors of the bench. The shadows are deep and black. We're swimming, but the darkness is encroaching. It's a dialectic between fun and anger. There it is—the summer of 'twenty. We were scared. We were happy. We were angry.

I've always thought art is a spiritual discipline, because it forces one to look closer at the world. Here is the question saving me right now: What is most beautiful about this moment, and how can I display it? Artists ask this question best. Most of us would do well to sit with an artist for a day and ask them to teach us to open our eyes. These are our spiritual teachers who are trained to sit in front of a standard vase and show us that it's not just a vase; it's angles and light and shades. It can have a feeling—happy, sad, lonely. Artists are dissatisfied with the mundane because, to them, the mundane doesn't exist. Everything is brimming with beauty. And then, these instructors of optometry bestow us with a greater reverence for life.

I'm not sure it's natural to pay attention to the world. Indeed, much of life has a way of becoming monotonous and dull. Everything is fine, but nothing is new. Quarantine, in particular, put a gray filter on the world so that reality looked like every apocalyptic movie ever made. Never thought I'd live in a chapter of Cormac McCarthy's *The Road*. But there we were, with days that fused to create an eternal Monday. Every day was the same as the last, which would be the same as the next. My senses no longer expected to be surprised.[1]

Quotidian routines can suck the life right out of us like a dementor. I'd be glad to let someone save me from my nightly chores: bathing the kids, getting them in bed, making lunches, and premaking the coffee. Nothing surprises me or stops me in my tracks. Is that because I don't expect to encounter something beautiful?

And if it's not the monotony of life, then the pendulum will swing too far in the opposite direction. We're a busy people, so we can fool ourselves into thinking we're an important people—a happy people. If the entire world is an art gallery, most of us rush to the next painting without stopping to look at the one right in front of our eyes. Busyness is the most trivial means of creating one's world to escape the world we inhabit; we are alienated from beauty.

Ludwig Wittgenstein challenges us to recover a distinctive mode of looking at the world—as in his famous injunction, "To repeat: don't think, but look!"[2] What can teach me to stop and contemplate the world?

Amateur photography is my current method of watchfulness. It's my newest way to share praise, thankfulness, or lament without even using any words. As many others have said, art is the language of the soul, making it a kind of prayer. We bypass the need to use our words or rationality to capture the hard day, express awe, or just find beauty and meaning in the mundane. I do not know what I ought to pray, so the Spirit intercedes with every wordless click.

Spiritualists might name the practice *visio divina*, or divine seeing. It's a way of granting God access to the heart by turning down the volume in the brain and opening our eyes a little wider. There is an imperative in the Christian life to be attentive, after all, to look twice at the things the world ignores.

Attention is a muscle that must be exercised. Maybe the place to start is with a pencil. A paintbrush will work, too. While I've found that incessant cell phone use is an escape from reality, I discovered that intentionally carrying a camera a couple of times a week has helped me to watch the world a little more closely, tuning my senses in to the wonder and depth and feelings in everyday life. The camera is a mnemonic device to stay bright-eyed enough to notice the colors, shapes, and textures around me. Nothing is posed, because life does not need to be posed. There's enough beauty without telling people how and where to stand.

I guess it's better to say that one makes pictures. In every moment, there's a relationship between the person and the object—the perceiver and the perceived. But it's never as simple as apprehending something waiting to be taken. It's an encounter. Together, you make something that might have otherwise been missed.

There are a multitude of stories unfolding in every moment. And I'm learning how to piece each moment into the story I want to tell—that the world, indeed, is beautiful.

· · · · · · · · · · · · · · · · ✦ · · · · · · · · · · · · · · · · ·

"I believe the world will be saved by beauty," said Prince Lev Nikolayevich Myshkin in Fyodor Dostoevsky's *The Idiot*. I'm not sure if it's true, but it sounds right.

I do know that when the world is at its ugliest, it's all the more important to cling to beauty. For instance, you might walk into work on a Tuesday morning, meet with a woman who needs to use the chapel for class, counsel a young man through relationship problems, and walk out three hours later without a job. You'll have no idea how to pay the bills or feed the children.

This is hypothetical, of course, but you can never be sure it won't happen to you.

Life is hard. So what do we do? We create. Most of us need to be saved by something, and beauty might do the trick. It must account for one reason why good art always follows tragedy and pain. Van Gogh painted *The Starry Night* amid manic depression; U2 got off the ground after the death of Bono's mother; Milton took pen to paper after losing his wife, daughter, and eyesight. Today, we reap the beauty of their brokenness.

When I lost my job, I woke up every morning to write. This helped me think less about the legality of using medieval torture devices. "*Illegitimi non carborundum*," I told myself. "Don't let the bastards grind you down." And I realized that the best weapon against the bastards is beauty. Otherwise, I knew I would become as ugly as those who stole my soul.

Every day, I had a fresh start—a white page, a cup of coffee. It was a moment of limitless potential; I could not say what would come or where I would be taken or surprised. I was lost in beauty for a couple of hours every morning until it released me into the world with new priorities.

A white page can be intimidating. Every morning, I wondered what would happen if nothing showed up. Writing is rarely romantic. Most often, she's a lousy date. She shows up late and never talks. But there would be a first word like the first stroke on a canvas or the glob of clay thrown on the wheel. I grabbed the first idea that darted from here to there and pinned it down. It was a starting place. I looked for the second and the third and the fourth until something took shape. Fragments would be joined together, and it would feel seemingly random until it wasn't. There is nothing, then something. It's *ex nihilo*, or out of nothing—almost.

Amid the formlessness, God hovered over the chaos and gave purpose and shape to the world. The page, like my life, was blank but tilled for creation. I could hear the opening chapter of Genesis resounding in my head, "And God saw that it was good." Or, to translate it differently, "And God saw that it was beautiful."

Is this how beauty saves us?

Shortly after Prince Myshkin pronounces that beauty will save the world, he is asked, "But which beauty?"

Supreme Court Justice Potter Steward said he wasn't sure how to define pornography, but he could recognize it when he saw it. Maybe beauty is like that. I think of a sunset's deep oranges and pinks that blend like watercolors. The tables are brimming with wine and overflowing with laughter. But beauty is also more than puppies and blades of grass. Could it be that beauty isn't always immediately apparent—that it isn't objective?

We're supposed to gaze in wonder at Renaissance art, but when I look at the *Mona Lisa*, I see a woman with an awkward smile. I haven't been given eyes to see the painting. Others say that a beautiful evening is sitting on the couch with a glass of wine while Mozart spins on the turn table.

That might be true. But it helps if you've taken courses on music theory and spent money on wine tastings. *The Tree of Life* by Terrence Malick was either stunning or stunningly dull, depending on what was going on in your life. Often, beauty is shaped by the glasses you put over your eyes and the aids you have installed in your ears.

"Beauty is in the eye of the beholder," they say. The person who is doing the looking must be taken into the equation. Beauty only makes sense in light of the stories and narratives that have taught us about the world. Pope Benedict XVI, the theologian formerly known as Joseph Ratzinger, once noted that you can be sure you have experienced the beautiful when you've experienced personal communication.[3] The Greek word for beauty, *kallos*, is a derivative of the word *kaleo*, which means "call." Art speaks to us. It peers into our souls, calls out our true name, and we answer.

What sort of beauty will save the world? Symmetry or balance or equivalence? A nose that is proportionate to the face? Eyes that are perfectly symmetrical? Darwinian aesthetics reduce beauty to evolutionary impulses for survival—the waterfall that's the very sustenance of life or the facial features that instill desire from a mate.

The parameters of beauty will depend on the story you are telling. Often, beauty is hijacked by ugly stories that are in the business of dealing with death. Beauty is deeply rooted in the auction block, where human beings were taught to interpret beauty based on a body's color, usefulness, and ability to generate capital. The cosmetic industry continues to orient a vision of beauty that excludes flaws. Why do you look so tired today? Maybe because you're not trying to conceal yourself. These standards continue to be passed down through people like Tyra Banks on *America's Next Top Model*. Beauty will save some. And it might damn others.

If the person you see in the mirror isn't extraordinarily beautiful, you are beholding a broken story.

Christianity tells a different story about beauty grounded in God's very own being. God is not an abstract principle or doctrine; God is beauty. And the faith is a particular training in the beautiful—it's a certain way of looking at the world that is not first nature. It's not that the world reveals something about God, but the opposite. God reveals something about the world we don't instinctively behold. As Richard Niebuhr says, conversion is a new way of seeing. When we encounter God, our senses become invigorated with the light of Christ so that we might see, feel, hear, touch, and perceive the world in all its beauty.

This is why Jesus constantly tried to reinvigorate the sensory life of people gathered on mountaintops and lakeside. "Do you have eyes and fail to see? Do you have ears and fail to hear?" he said (Mark 8:18). Beauty was rarely obvious. The kingdom of God? It's the seed. I promise the seed. It's the humble, the grieving, the poor, and the meek that are blessed. Look again, Jesus says.

Jesus asked Peter, James, and John to join him on a walk to the top of Mount Tabor, where things get weird (see: trippy). We call this the story of Christ's transfiguration—a word meaning "a change of form" and a course that can be taken for credit at Hogwarts School of Witchcraft and Wizardry. There is a dazzling light. Garments are as white as snow. The veil between heaven and earth is pulled back. Time stops. There is silence. Moses and Elijah appear next to Jesus, standing in for the Jewish law and the prophets. Jesus fulfills both.

Is this a hallucination? Sometimes, it's hard to tell the difference between whether you have foraged bad mushrooms or experienced the revelation of God. Maybe both can be true.

Most of us have experienced something like a transfiguration—well, maybe not dazzling light, ghosts, and voices from heaven. But we've had moments transfigured when time becomes different, otherworldly, even. It's the kind of moment where everything in the world feels right. Welcoming a newborn child to the world is one of these moments. Another occurs when Duke University beats the University of North Carolina in March Madness. Time's relentless marching stops for a cigarette break. And something feels holy.

"It's good to be here," says Peter.

"Let's put up some shacks."

"This moment doesn't have to end."

"We can stay here."

Have you ever tried to capture a moment? It's futile. Moments can't be contained any more than a picture can capture your mother's smell. That piece of frozen cake in your freezer will not allow you to relive your wedding day. The vial full of water from the Jordan River will not give you the moment when your feet sink into the mud at the riverbank. All moments, especially the holiest ones, will eventually come to an end.

Jesus asks the disciples to walk down the mountain and return to the world. He tells them it won't be full of rainbows and sunshine. There, at the foot of the mountain, a grieving father was looking for healing for his deeply ill child. And that father was waiting to see whether a transfiguration was possible. Further down the road, there was a cross and a tomb. Jesus had recently taught them that the Son of Man must suffer greatly at the hands of the leaders and chief priests and that he'd be put to death on the third day. At best, Jesus was a lousy Messiah. At worst, he's a liar and a fraud.

Peter loses his temper and says, "God forbid it."

Jesus rebukes him.

The One who shines in glory is the One who is marching toward death. Is God present there, too? Can the cross in the valley be as beautiful as the light on top of the mountain?

The journey from the transfiguration to the cross fractures all our neat, settled narratives of beauty that rest on harmony, clarity, and symmetry. Karl Barth puts it this way: "At the Transfiguration, we see that divine beauty embraces death as well as life, fear as well as joy, what we might call the ugly as well as what we might call the beautiful."[4] The cross becomes beautiful, and not because the carpenters get the geometry right, but because it reveals the depth of God's love. God enters our pain, God knows rejection, and God suffers anguish.

I know many people who find beauty in sunsets and fewer who willingly enter suffering to experience something of the presence and beauty of God. Refugee houses, homeless shelters, and war zones don't top our lists of "most beautiful places to visit." But God is also emptied into the world's worst hells, that there may be no place where God is absent. Carl Jung tells this story handed down from the rabbis: A student asked a rabbi why no one saw God anymore, and the rabbi answered, "Because nowadays no one is willing to stoop so low!"[5] We look up to a God who is supposed to be on the mountain and then trip over the Christ in the valley. Those glimpses that are not "conventionally pleasing" can also be beautiful, but they might require a trained eye. There is beauty in life or death, but our senses must undergo the proper training to perceive it.

Spread mud on our eyes, O Jesus, and teach us to see again.

✦

Sam Wells, a theologian and priest for the Church of England, is known to say, "If it can't be happy, make it beautiful." We make a mistake when we conflate beauty with happiness. Some situations will never be good. Nor will they be pretty. But most can become beautiful. Barbara Brown Taylor writes that these moments have a particular kind of beauty: "They are beautiful in the sense of labor and delivery. They are beautiful in the sense of a white flag over a still-smoking battlefield. They are beautiful in the sense of the first bird to land on the lifeboat with something green in its beak. You were lost and now are found, and beauty is all around."[6]

There is a legend that the cross burst into flowers at the first Easter. God, the gardener, took an instrument of torture and death and transformed it into a blooming instrument of salvation. If beauty is to save the world, it must be this beauty. The kind of beauty that can change us from the inside out. The kind that will move us from looking at mountains to moving mountains. From hearing a song to playing a new song. It's the kind that will embrace the labor pains until a beautiful new child is born.

A Prayer of Illumination

Awaken my eyes
to see the world as if for the first time.
Stir up my heart
to fall in love again.
Quicken my imagination
to bend moments.
Move my fingers
to tell what cannot be told.
And hold the world in lines.

Train me to look at the world
with my eyes—
a challenge to objectivity.
And also reveal the world to me
in a way I could not see
before my eyes were opened and
ears unplugged,
that I may become
an optometrist for humanity.

My work is the language of the soul
expressed through lines and dots
angles and light.
Make my joy, tangible.
My cries, a beautiful song.
And my work,
a prayer.

There's a story unfolding out of every moment.
Help me to tell the story with
Beauty.

Singing Who We Will Be

One of today's most controversial street artists is Banksy, an anonymous street artist and political activist. I like to think of him as the anti-Batman, a masked vigilante fighting crime with spray paint. One of his more well-known pieces, *Love Is in the Air,* appeared in Bethlehem shortly after the construction of the West Bank Wall between Palestine and Israel. Banksy had long been active in the area, calling attention to the terrorism and militarism throughout the Israeli-Palestinian conflict. This particular piece of graffiti depicts a protestor, wearing a baseball cap and a bandana to mask the lower half of his face, hurling a Molotov cocktail at his enemies. But with Banksy, things are not always as they seem. Instead of a Molotov cocktail, he throws a bouquet of colorful flowers.

Banksy operates in a long tradition that believes art has the power to disrupt the accepted order of the world. It can make us stop in our tracks and look twice at the unchecked norms and values.

Wait, is that protestor hurling flowers?

It's absurd to throw flowers during a war.

No. War is absurd when you live in a world with flowers.

And so, Banksy helps us see that the antidote to bombs is not more bombs, just as the answer to hatred must not be more hatred. Instead, the solution to the ugliness of the world must be beauty.

Christians have long known that we answer the darkness of the world with a great light. When the Nazis first invaded Poland at the beginning of World War II, a university student named Karol Wojtyla founded a theater. Some resisted the brute force of the Nazis by fighting, willingly facing death by throwing themselves against the strength of the military. Others risked arrest by smuggling theater sets into living rooms and enacting a different way of being in the world. Wojtyla, who would later become Pope John Paul II, knew that when Orpheus sings a more beautiful song, who bothers to listen to the voices of the sirens?

Friedrich Nietzsche, one of the great Christian sparring partners, said, "They will have to sing better songs before I believe in their redeemer."[1] During Christmas, we get out our instruments, warm up our voices, and take our best shot. In the church, Christmas is a season so beautiful that we can't explain it with words. We sing. And it began with Mary, Mother of God, singing for revolution.

We encounter Mary in the first chapter of Luke when the angel Gabriel was sent to her to announce the birth of our Savior, Jesus Christ. Mary was young. She might have been twelve—thirteen—fourteen years old. Some scholars say twenty. Most agree that she was also poor. Worst of all? Mary was engaged in planning a wedding. Despite this, Gabriel approaches Mary and tells her she is favored. Gabriel tells Mary her life is about to change—drastically. Her body and her life would become a house for God. She's a kid tasked with giving birth to the Savior of the cosmos. It's weird—something only God would choose to do.

Pregnancy is full of excitement and wonder but also a season of fear. Mary placed her hope in flesh and blood vessels and cells that need to divide and grow. She was held hostage to a bundle of cells and a God she couldn't control. The world's hopes and fears were bound in a tiny package marked "fragile."

And so, Mary did what many pregnant women do—she found an older relative for support. She climbed on her camel and traveled alone for seventy miles to visit her cousin Elizabeth. Two women gathered, one too old and one too young, both bearing children that will make all things new. At a loss for words, they sing a song:

> My soul magnifies the Lord,
>   and my spirit rejoices in God my Savior,
> for he has looked with favor on the lowly state of his servant.
>   Surely from now on all generations will call me blessed,
> for the Mighty One has done great things for me,
>   and holy is his name;
> indeed, his mercy is for those who fear him
>   from generation to generation.
> He has shown strength with his arm;
>   he has scattered the proud in the imagination of their hearts.
> He has brought down the powerful from their thrones
>   and lifted up the lowly;
> he has filled the hungry with good things,
>   and sent the rich away empty.
> He has come to the aid of his child Israel,
>   in remembrance of his mercy,
> according to the promise he made to our ancestors,
>   to Abraham and to his descendants forever. (Luke 1:46-55)

Pregnant parents are told their children can hear their voices in the womb. Therefore, when their children are born, they can recognize their voices. I've noticed that some children listen to us for nine months in the womb to figure out which voice to ignore for the rest of their lives. Still, we exit the womb familiar with the lullabies we heard while sloshing around the amniotic fluid.

But the Magnificat is not a lullaby. It's a remix of Hannah's song from the Hebrew Scriptures, passed down among the Hebrew people. She puts a new beat to an old tune. Mary (Miriam, meaning "the rebellion") sings of a God who burns the world down to its foundation—char and ash. God rebuilds the world upside down. It's revolution, an indictment of the corrupt and liberation for the oppressed.

Mary's song uproots the status quo by dreaming of a new social order where the poor give alms to the rich. And the kings sit on the street corners begging for food from people experiencing homelessness. The humble and meek rise to the company's top, while the proud are left at the bottom, begging for vacation time. It's a crazy, laughable vision. But the song Jesus hears in the womb becomes his life's music.

Andrew Fletcher, an eighteenth-century Scottish politician, once said, "If a man were permitted to make all the ballads, he need not care who should make the laws of a nation."[2] The song Mary sings creates an imaginative space for resistance; she is a menace to conformity and a threat to political dictators.[3] That's why Guatemala outlawed the public reading of Mary's song in the 1980s. This song is so catchy that people might take it seriously and try overthrowing the government. A few years ago, the Russian punk rock band Pussy Riot entered Christ the Savior Cathedral in Moscow. They walked to the front of the sanctuary, invaded the altar space, and began to sing at the top of their lungs,

> Virgin Mary, Mother of God, put Putin away.
> put Putin away, put Putin away.

Music, while often tender and sentimental, can also be a scathing prophetic critique. To paraphrase Picasso, every act of creation is first a destruction.[4]

Paintings, sculptures, and songs can slip right past our defense mechanisms to hit us in the gut. Herbert Marcuse, a philosopher, says, "The truth of art lies in its power to break the monopoly of established reality to define what is real."[5] It can be a means of what Simone Weil calls "attention"—transcending oneself to see and hear things more clearly and as they are—to experience the world through another person's eyes or listen to it through their ears.

Many Christians are well acquainted with Dietrich Bonhoeffer—the pastor, theologian, secret agent, and martyr—known for an assassination attempt on Hitler. Fewer Christians are familiar with the experiences that coalesced into his resistance. One such experience is the year Bonhoeffer spent in the United States at Union Theological Seminary. While studying at Union, he spent his time worshipping at Harlem's famed Abyssinian Baptist Church under the leadership of Adam Clayton Powell. Here, Bonhoeffer learned, particularly through song, that Jesus was not the God of Empire. The God of Israel is the God who suffers.

One day after church, Bonhoeffer, who was often dispassionate and cold, came home emotional from singing the African American spirituals of the church. His friend later recalled, "Perhaps that Sunday afternoon . . . I witnessed a beginning of his identification with the oppressed, which played a role in the decision that led to his death."[6] Bonhoeffer encountered Christ anew when he sang the songs of African Americans who had been enslaved, lynched, and freed from their chains. Here is Christ who suffered with the outcast and marginalized—a Black Christ who suffered with African Americans in a White supremacist world.

In the presence of a new song, Bonhoeffer decentered a European theology. He realized that the Christ we worship had been transfigured into an ethereal European, distanced from his Palestinian roots and divorced from the coarseness of his life, the scars implanted into his hands. Jesus cannot be rendered with deep blue eyes or brown flowing locks. Having heard the music of the African American church, Bonhoeffer could no longer close his ears to the cries of the Jewish people. The spirituals he experienced at Abyssinian became the soundtrack to his resistance to the Nazi atrocities when most Christians in Germany rushed to arms to fight alongside Hitler.

Marcuse reminds us, "Art doesn't change the world, but it may change the consciousness of people who can change the world."[7] And that's why we must sing songs we do not write. Joining another's song reminds us that we are in God's symphony, not our own, and we leave more connected to everything and everyone around us. Art isn't helpful when it tells us what we already know in the language we already speak. But when it reveals a side of the world we couldn't apprehend, it can be a foretaste of heaven and an instrument of its fulfillment.

A former professor calls the songs and poems of Scripture the poetry of the impossible, which is opposed to the prose of the probable.[8] It's significant because it shows us what could be but is not yet. Against all odds, we believe Christ can topple the kingdom of this world. It makes no sense.

But Christians are a people of the impossible because we are a people of resurrection. The impossible poetry of Easter is that the stone has been rolled away and the dead are now alive. What is possible won't save us, so we must sing the songs of resurrection—the songs of the impossible.

The violence, the ugliness, the grief of the world threaten to steal voices and render us mute. But the church dares to gather. What can we do?

We can sing a song of defiance.

Once you've learned the song, you'll never get it out of your head. You can't help but sing it everywhere you go. We get out of the pew. We sing about Jesus's work of liberation.

· · · · · · · · · · · · · · · · ✦ · · · · · · · · · · · · · · · · ·

A renowned concert pianist was starting a performance when suddenly a mother screamed in the audience. A child had gotten up from her seat and was running around the auditorium. At this instant, the pianist left his seat at the piano to see what the commotion was all about. Suddenly, the child ran up on the stage, sat on the piano stool, and began pecking at random keys. The audience gasped in horror.

Unexpectedly, the pianist walked toward the child and stood behind her. Then, the pianist leaned over the child and placed his two hands outside of the child's hands. The pianist began to play in response to the child's notes and created an improvised melody. Amid the chaos, they created a song.

There will always be discord in the world. But God gives us scales to work with: love, hope, peace. Try to lean on those scales. God provides us with a band to lean on. Trust each other—and the music we are making—and God will improvise a song.[9]

THREE

SACRED STORIES

A Genesis
Our First Stories

The world was created through words. God could have fashioned the Earth with God's hands, like a potter who picks up clay and throws it on the wheel, adds water, and applies pressure. Other creation myths speak of irritated gods that create the heavens and the earth by splitting a corpse in half. But the God of Israel used a poetic story to speak the world into existence—a word, "light," to set it all in motion. "Let there be a dome," said God. "And lights in the sky. Let there be swarms of living creatures—birds that fly above the earth, creeping things, and wild animals" (see Genesis 1). Story is performative; it creates. It shapes reality by telling us who we are and ought to become.

We misuse our words when we assume they don't have the power to give life. Certain words will change things. You are given a name, bestowing an identity. A judge hits the gavel, and you're innocent. The priest pronounces a marriage, and you become one flesh. Each of these words are creative in nature.

The family and the nation exist because there is a past and a future, both of which are comprised of the stories we believe and want to believe—the stories we manufacture and the stories we try to forget. Can a romantic relationship exist without stories of the first date, the first promise, the first argument? Your life has meaning because there is a beginning, and there will be an ending. In the middle, there will be a story.

If there is no story, there is no meaning.

One of the first things I do in a person's house is make my way to their bookshelves. There is great intimacy in perusing the stories a person gives permanent residence in their home. The words bound between two covers reveal something of a person's beginning and end—and what they believe they ought to squeeze in between their own two great flaps.

The books on display aren't often arbitrary; this is especially true for people who have moved. These aren't just the stories they have read and reread; they are the stories they have kept because the stories have kept them. What genres are present? What's well-worn and what's never been opened? Which page corners are bent? Or maybe it's the case that they have cardboard boxes from Anthropology that are manufactured to look like books (these are the kinds of people who care more about having money than the stories that tell them how to use their money).

Not everyone reads, and that is their loss. Still, their bookshelves will contain other treasured stories: their grandfather's American flag received at his funeral, a mother's desk name plate, a quote on a woodblock from a book one ought to read but never will, a souvenir from the most crucial trip of her life. There might be physical and digital bookshelves full of movies and stories told through moving pictures. Our stories are all around us—the books and trinkets and gifts and mementos. To others, they might not mean anything. To you, they contain covert directions, shortcuts to find your way back to yourself, reminding you when to turn, speed up, or slow down. They inform you when you've made a wrong turn. When you're lost, the story is your direction home.

When my Pappy died, my Memaw got rid of most of his books, as well as his papers and sermons. Without his library, I lost access to his identity.

I've often thought about what he underlined in his books. What did he write in the margins of his favorite texts? When Pappy's dementia grew worse, he picked up the newspaper and underlined important phrases and paragraphs—a habit that was ingrained in his muscle memory after years of reading and studying.

There was his death. And there was the death of his stories. His death felt more permanent when his stories were given away.

My childhood home was always cluttered with books. They were on tables (and under them); they were on shelves and stacked in piles next to beds. What does this say about us? We kept our best friends within arm's reach. Some might be dead, but their blood still courses through the ink. And whenever we open their books, their hearts beat, and we're reconnected.

I suspect that another reason we kept our stories close is because we loved sharing them with others. When we share a book with another, we also share a part of ourselves. I can't remember a time when my mom wasn't moving books from the shelf to her bedside table or into another person's hands. Still today, we are patrons of her library, grabbing books off her shelf and returning others, asking for new reviews about the latest bestsellers.

One of the first books my mom shared with us was *The Story of Ferdinand*. We read it often before bedtime, tucked under her arms. It was a story of a gentle beast who spent his time smelling flowers under his favorite cork tree despite the herd of bulls playing roughly just across the field.

One day, he sat on a bee. The bee, under the weight of fifteen hundred pounds, stung Ferdinand. He jumped up, bucked his legs, snorted, and stomped. Ferdinand was mistaken for a fighter and forced into the ring with the most powerful matadors in Spain. Since it was not in his nature to fight, he chose to sit quietly in the middle of the field, catching the scent of the flowers drifting through the field from women's hats.

I can't say whether I enjoyed hearing the story. I'm not sure it matters. Ferdinand was on my bookshelf, and I had to wrestle with becoming the kind of person who pays attention to those who sit under cork trees.

· · · · · · · · · · · · · ✦ · · · · · · · · · · · · ·

When the Hebrew people talk about the future, they ironically use a word that means "behind," *qetem*. The future is that which is behind you. On the other hand, the Hebrew people talked about the past with the word *aharit*, which means "future." Your past is always in front of you. And you can only walk into the future if you are facing backward, with your eyes and ears tuned to the stories that came before you.

The most important story my parents shared with me was the story of Jesus. My parents were deeply Christian—my mom was the kind of Christian who taught children's Sunday school, who asked us to memorize Scripture and learn the order of the books of the Bible. She rarely talked much about her faith; we inferred its importance by how often she took us to church. My siblings and I knew we would be in church every Sunday, regardless of the length and volume of the best tantrum we could muster.

I've never entirely understood why some parents want to let their young children make up their minds about things like faith and ultimate reality. "We don't indoctrinate our children," some parents divulge proudly. Of course, they are wrong. Meanwhile, they sit their kids down on the couch and tell them all kinds of sacred stories about presidents, hobbits, celebrities, or pop stars—or they will make you watch the Georgia Bulldogs or the Fighting Illini. Dressed in Duke blue, you learn to shout, "Go to hell, Carolina, go to hell." We have no identity apart from those who tell us our most formative stories, and we hold no self that exists before and unencumbered by the social relations that shape our identity. To try to avoid teaching a story is to teach a story.

It was only natural that we would be Christians, too.

God's stories, like any other story, must be told. We must hear from God before we can speak to God. Throughout most of history, God's stories were heard and heard only. Most people of God haven't had the luxury of owning a Bible, much less knowing how to read it. This was especially true for the Hebrew people. One of the most important Jewish scriptures, prayed every morning and every night, goes like this, "Hear O Israel: The LORD is our God, the LORD alone. You shall love the LORD your God with all your heart and with all your soul and with all your might" (Deut. 6:4–5). This scripture is called the *Shema*, or "hear."

If there is no hearing, there will be no doing.

And so, God told the Israelites to learn the story and pass it down through each generation. When your children ask you who you are or why you live the way you live, tell them the story: "We were Pharaoh's slaves in Egypt, but the LORD brought us out of Egypt with a mighty hand" (Deut. 6:21). Every Passover, Jewish children ask, "How is tonight unlike any other night?" And the parents tell them the story: They tried to kill us. We survived. Let's eat.

The people who loved me most wanted me to hear this story, too. They dragged me to "big church" every Sunday morning to listen to sermons I didn't care to understand. But there were Sunday school classes and vacation Bible schools—where strangers bothered to learn my name and hand out unethically sourced crafts that didn't survive the car ride home. The story was our least common denominator, our only reason for being together.

I was a kid in the church in the late eighties and early nineties, so I grew up with felt Bible figures and flannel boards (remember, these were the days before Bible characters became fruits and vegetables). The world was created there, on a flannel board. Adam and Eve hid behind felt trees after they disobeyed God. Felt Abraham was raised out of Ur, and Joseph was clothed in a felt coat of many colors. Felt animals boarded a felt ark. A felt river was divided so that Moses could lead his felt people into freedom.

I now wonder if this is the right way to read the Scriptures. Instead of breaking down the narrative into constituent parts to locate meaning, the story was enacted—a playground for the imagination. The story wasn't ruined by pinning down its meaning once and for all, and the point of the story could not be extracted from the story itself. The Book, in other words, was not just a way to learn more about God; it was a place to encounter God and us in a story.

Alasdair MacIntyre said, "I can only answer the question 'What am I to do?' if I can answer the prior question 'Of what story or stories do I find myself a part?'"[1] My life is incomprehensible without that story. I knew Jesus before I knew myself, and I do not know myself apart from his story. There is no way to peel back the layers and discover a self that Jesus has not in some way touched. I know that my life began with Adam, was liberated by God through Moses, and was refined through the prophets. As a child, I learned that I wasn't just a Snider. I also belonged to God, and salvation is accepting the story as autobiography. One day, I could choose to sever the relationship, but I couldn't remove the story from my DNA.

And that's partly what it means to be created. To be created is to receive the gift of being storied. None of us chose to be born. Nor did we choose our parents or whether we'd have siblings. But we gradually find who we are when we spend time hearing the stories. And now, when I look in the mirror, I don't just see myself. I behold stories that have made me who I am.

Some of the stories we inherit will be fairy tales with happy endings, but others will be full of horror and suspense. You might decide to take some books off your shelf and replace them with better, more beautiful stories. You may even decide to take the Bible off the shelf for a while so that one day, you can decide whether to put it back on. But before we can critically evaluate our stories, we must first hear them.

When ancient priests baptized new converts, they touched the ears of the person raised to new life and said the Aramaic word, "Ephphatha." It's the same word Jesus used to open the ears of the deaf.

In other words, listen.

· · · · · · · · · · · · · · · · ✦ · · · · · · · · · · · · · · · ·

Flannery O'Connor said, "Don't let me ever think, dear God, that I was anything but the instrument for Your story—just like the typewriter was mine."[2] I suspect that a story that isn't grafted into a larger story is not much of a story. I often wonder whether my life is hitting the right keys and what lines I am contributing to God's grand narrative.

I once presided at the funeral of a carpenter who lived to be ninety years old. As a carpenter, he was the kind of man who could look at ordinary objects and perceive their potential. This is not natural for all people. When I look at a piece of wood, I see a piece of wood. This man looked at wood and saw cabinets, tables, houses, and elaborately carved bowls. The wood is what it is, and it is what it can become. His profession was of potentiality and transformation.

Maybe this is why carpentry was Jesus's profession. We aren't told much about the first thirty years of Jesus's life, so we must imagine how he spent his time. Years working with stone and wood, hammer and saw. His hands were worn—splintered, blistered, and dirty. Some take this to mean he had bulging biceps; he was a man's man. Others note the way it explains his life and ministry. Jesus was a carpenter because he spent his time transforming. God knows that our world can be carved into something beautiful, so our God sent us Jesus Christ to carve all of us into what only God can imagine.

The carpenter in my congregation never missed a Sunday morning or a Wednesday evening at the church. I suspect this is why he squeezed my hand as I read him Scripture while he took his last breaths. His family and I prayed over him, trusting that his final transformation was underway.

At his funeral, I told the story of two carpenters. Funerals are where the church tries to make sense of a person's life in light of the most important story of their lives. But at the end of the funeral, we walked outside to the graveside escorted by men in military uniform. The trumpets blew, the guns were fired, and the flag was folded and handed to the widow. A country can ask you to die, but it cannot raise you from the grave. There's a stoic acceptance of the finality of death and honor for a courageous life. The cognitive dissonance always makes me uncomfortable.

Which story gets the last word on someone's life? Only a Carpenter can take a wooden box, raise it, and create a tree. I suppose that's the most important story.

This is one of the reasons why a riot almost broke out at the funeral of the philosopher and theologian Søren Kierkegaard. He was buried according to the wrong story.

The religious officials weren't sure what to do with Kierkegaard when he died. Kierkegaard was a fierce critic of the national church, which he declared had been absorbed into the nation's identity (and not the other way around). He wrote, "We are what is called a 'Christian' nation—but in such a sense that not a single one of us is in the character of the Christianity of the New Testament."[3] He sought to heighten the demand of the religion by making it more difficult to be a Christian than merely exiting a Dutch womb. We must also subjectively choose to affirm the stories we inherit.

Here's Kierkegaard's question: If everyone is born a Christian, is anyone a Christian?

Kierkegaard wrote that the greatest enemy of Christianity was not its scathing critics, atheists, or scoffers. No, its worst enemy was a church that made religion into a hobby, with neither cost nor pain. Kierkegaard once compared the church to a beer seller who sold the stuff just below the cost of producing it. They might sell a hell of a lot of beer, but they'll go broke in the end. The church sold a knock-off Jesus—a Jesus that is procured for half the cost from a man's briefcase on the corner of a busy street. Kierkegaard hadn't stepped foot in a church in over a year before his death because he knew the actual price of Christianity.

And so, it was odd that Kierkegaard was wrapped in the Danish flag and laid on the ground by the people he called liars and deceivers. Kierkegaard's nephew denounced that he was buried in this manner (amid the ladies in red and blue hats and a dog in a muzzle) by stating, "In the name of God, one moment, Gentlemen, permit me." Henrik Lund, the nephew, continued, "He, my deceased friend, stands and falls with his writings, but I have not heard them mentioned with a single word . . . this funeral is a crime against honesty, a crime reserved for official Christianity to commit."[4]

The national church wouldn't absorb Kierkegaard's story into their own. With scattered applause, Søren was laid into the mud.

Kierkegaard may not have called himself a Christian, but he was obsessed with becoming one. Jesus's story was the only one, the meta-narrative by which Kierkegaard chose to live and die. But he also knew that Jesus ought to cost something. Kierkegaard's life, then, was inexplicable—full of great suffering. He lost his respectability, his relationships, and his reputation. None of his contemporaries understood how he could throw away so much potential, but he knew that a well-lived life must be a confounding, wasteful one.

After Kierkegaard died, they found the words he requested be placed on his tombstone. It's this poem:

Just a short while,
then I have won.
Then, the whole struggle entirely disappears.
Then I can rest in halls of roses
and talk with my Jesus without ceasing.[5]

Everyone jostles for the power to tell you who you are. Who are you? An American? A carpenter? A consumer? A Democrat?

When you are put under the ground, what story will you choose to cover you?

◆

I recently started reading the Chronicles of Narnia series with my daughter. Before we walked through the wardrobe into an enchanted land with fauns, witches, lions, and Turkish delight, we read the dedication of *The Lion, the Witch, and the Wardrobe* from the author, C. S. Lewis, to his goddaughter, Lucy:

> My Dear Lucy,
>
> I wrote this story for you, but when I began it I had not realized that girls grow quicker than books. As a result you are already too old for fairy tales, and by the time it is printed and bound you will be older still. But some day you will be old enough to start reading fairy tales again. You can then take it down from some upper shelf, dust it, and tell me what you think of it. I shall probably be too deaf to hear, and too old to understand, a word you say, but I shall still be your affectionate Godfather.[6]

Somewhere along the way, we forget how to read stories. Joy is lost to rationality. We accrue Enlightenment-shaped burdens of historicity, archaeological evidence, and cosmology. The story becomes a problem to solve rather than a mystery we should dwell within.

My daughter, who also recently became obsessed with Harry Potter, cornered me while driving her to school.

"Is it true?" she asked. "You know, Hogwarts. Is it a real place? And Hermione? Is she a real person? Is it a true story?"

I tried to tell her some stories are true because they are historically accurate and verifiable. Other stories are true even when there are no birth certificates or fossils or geological evidence. These stories say something about humanity, good and evil, or how we might find our place in the world. And that's an essential kind of truth.

ANCIENT EXTRAVAGANCE

Once, following a lecture on Genesis, a woman asked the theologian Karl Barth if there was a literal serpent in the garden of Eden that spoke. Barth responded, "Madame, it matters not if the serpent actually spoke. What matters is what the serpent said."

This summer, my daughter and I are reading the third book in the Chronicles of Narnia series, *The Voyage of the Dawn Treader*. In one of my favorite scenes, Lucy Pevensie and her friends are taken captive by the dufflepuds on an island while looking for the lost lords of Narnia. The dufflepuds were simple creatures—dwarfs, really. They hopped around on one foot each, suffering from a spell that made them invisible. And so it goes that these duffers wouldn't allow Lucy and her friends to leave their island until they were made visible. Coerced and inspired to find the spell, Lucy happens upon the magician's quarters, locates the book of spells, and flips through the book of fascinating magic. She lands on the spell "for the refreshment of spirit." Lewis writes:

> And what Lucy found herself reading was more like a story than a spell. It went on for three pages and before she had read to the bottom of the page she had forgotten that she was reading at all. She was living in the story as if it were real, and all the pictures were real too. When she had got to the third page and come to the end, she said, "That is the loveliest story I've ever read or ever shall read in my whole life. Oh, I wish I could have gone on reading it for ten years. At least I'll read it over again." . . . And she never could remember; and ever since that day what Lucy means by a good story is a story which reminds her of the forgotten story in the Magician's Book.[7]

What is the loveliest story by which all other stories are judged? I have heard the loveliest story ever told, and I haven't been able to call another story good unless it reminded me of the first story—the one that has shaped all others. In the loveliest story, I received a history and a future that relegated all the other stories that clamored for my attention. In the present, I've found a lamp unto my feet and a light unto my path.

Seventy Faces of the Torah
Reading the Story

The Bible is an inherited story we must learn to read. A Reformation scholar, David Steinmetz, says we should read the Bible like a mystery novel. I know that seems sacrilegious for those who were taught that God is Father, Son, Holy Spirit, and Book. But the book is not God (contrary to some belief). Since the Bible is not God, it means it can, and probably should, be read like most other books. One of my favorite thinkers describes the Bible as a five-act drama: Creation, Israel, Jesus, Church, and New Creation.[1] It has plot, characters, and movements. There is a beginning and an end.

Of course, it can't be read exactly like all other books, especially if we believe God was breathing in and through the authors in some unique way. Here's what makes it even more complex: It's composed of multiple interrelated genres. Imagine if someone crammed a library full of Plato, Mary Oliver, and Bob Dylan into one book. That's the Bible. The Bible is all these things, and none of them entirely. It's a book. It's a library of books. It has poetry, but it's not a poem. It has rules for a life well-lived, but it is not an instruction manual. (It would be a lousy instruction book; it's vague, and sometimes it contradicts itself. Parts are missing, making it more complicated than IKEA furniture to put together.) There is history, but it is not a textbook as much as a communal diary. It has proverbs, but it is not some horoscope with pithy advice to get you through your day. It involves the natural world, but it's not a physics book.

There is no economy of words. The Bible is beautiful and sometimes wasteful, confusing but always extravagant in its narrative.

When I was at camp as a kid, I was asked what was most challenging about reading the Bible. I promptly answered that I couldn't understand a thing. "Paul is particularly irritating," I said. My counselor (condescendingly) told me to get a better translation. The translation wasn't the problem. The problem was animal sacrifices, ancient kings, a temple, and a man who says he is a temple. How do all these texts fit together? It's a mystery—sometimes enthralling and often nonsensical. A Tree of Life? Purity rituals? A big fish with indigestion? There are subplots and timelines that don't coordinate. Some stories are dead ends. Others are too foreign or boring to comprehend.

This is why Karl Barth called the Bible a strange new world, the world of God.[2] The Bible ought to feel odd if it tells the story of God. Anything that reveals God ought to be brimming with mystery. The Bible is mysterious, too, because it didn't belong to most of us—at least at first. It's been passed down through cultures, decades, and millennia. It should feel strange, especially to Gentiles, or those who are not Jewish; it wasn't our family story until Jesus adopted us into the group.

I had a teacher who shared this story: Imagine you showed up to church one Sunday and grabbed a pew Bible from the rack, but something was different about this Bible. The Bible didn't have a New Testament. It was, instead, the Old Testament, the Hebrew Bible—written in Hebrew. And, of course, you showed up without your Bible because you're a Methodist, and Methodists don't read the Bible. Nor can your pastors read Hebrew because they attended a mainline seminary. The congregation is gathered around a story no one can read or understand.

Someone in the congregation says, "I know a guy down the block, a Jewish guy, who can read this stuff." The problem is that no one knows this Jewish man. He's strange. He tells weird stories. Eats different food. They knock on the door and greet him. He's not quite presentable, but he agrees to come. He shows up, walks into the pulpit, and stands before these Christians to translate the Hebrew. For the next hour, everything depends on this man who is unlike you, but you need to understand God's Word. He is the master detective, like Sherlock Holmes or Miss Marple, who brings all the suspects, timelines, and spectators into a room and reveals all the mysteries of the text.[3]

It's an imperfect analogy, but it speaks to the importance of Jesus, a Jew who teaches Gentiles to read a story that is not theirs. If there is no Jesus, there is no story—at least for Gentiles. But in Jesus, the Scripture becomes a word about the Word for the whole world.

The mystery has been solved. We read the Scriptures through a Jesus-shaped lens. His birth, life, death, and resurrection give new life to all the other words of the book. He is the interpreter and the most important clue for the entire story. He is the one who should be placed at the center of the evidence board. All strings lead to him and from him.

In Jesus, the whole thing has to be reread, starting with the last chapter first. Then, you reread it, beginning with the first chapter. Every text takes on new dimensions and depth in light of Jesus. We are enslaved by sin, death, and evil; resurrection's dry land is on the other side of the cross. That's the exodus. How could we have overlooked that the Song of Songs can be read about God's love for the church? The ethnic cleansing of the Canaanites commanded by God was a dead end, never suggested by God. The story of the rape of Tamar? A cautionary tale. Why does God always save with wood? On the ark, in the bitter water at Marah, on the cross?

Look closer, reread the text, and you'll find countless Easter eggs spread throughout the narrative. No matter how many times I have read the text, there is always something new to unearth—new diamonds are constantly being created when the pressures of today encounter the fire of the Holy Spirit.

God slowly and patiently forms God's people through telling and retelling stories. This Book breathes new life into every generation.

Or maybe it's better to say that Scripture is not a mystery novel. I haven't made up my mind. Søren Kierkegaard once described the Bible as a love letter written in a foreign language. The Bible certainly feels like it was written in a foreign language; much of the letter evades our interpretation and exceeds our grasp. We, the beloved, desperately wanting to understand the words from the lover, will employ the best dictionaries and lexicons to translate the work. But the work of translation is a means to an end. If we spend too much time on translation, we are robbed of the love. The point of the letter is not to create a definitive history or a timeless ethic but to meditate on the words. To sink into the ink.

The Scriptures, then, are a living communication to encounter our beloved. In reading the love story, we experience the one who stands within and beyond it and ourselves. We find ourselves changed by the story on our way, becoming the kind of people who live according to a different story. God breathed when the authors wrote these words, but God is still breathing over the text and making it come alive. The authority of the Bible is in the encounter between the congregation and God through the Word, as God breathes and creates something new.

The Bible itself isn't this divine thing on its own, but when we read it together and the Spirit moves among us, the Bible facilitates an encounter with the living God.

⬩ ⬩ ⬩ ⬩ ⬩ ⬩ ⬩ ⬩ ⬩ ⬩ ⬩ ⬩ ⬩ ✦ ⬩ ⬩ ⬩ ⬩ ⬩ ⬩ ⬩ ⬩ ⬩ ⬩ ⬩ ⬩ ⬩

Annie Dillard recalls that once, in the middle of a long prayer, in a church on the island in Puget Sound, the pastor stopped and burst out, "Lord, we bring you these same petitions every week." He took a long pause, and then he continued with the prayer. Dillard wrote, "Because of this, I like him very much."[4]

Many of the church's rituals feel Sisyphean when we take them seriously enough to pay attention to them. We recite the same prayers, tell the same stories, year after year.

After year.

As best as I can tell, the stories aren't changing anytime soon. We tell the same variation of birth stories during Christmas. Some years later, we hear about Joseph, wise men, and the escape to Egypt. Other years, it's

Mary, Elizabeth, and shepherds. The resurrection story told at Easter is most often John's account. There's a gardener and a foot race. Spoiler: Every year, the tomb is empty. If you happen upon a church that structures its sermons through series, you're bound to hear "The Great Commission" once a year—maybe more. But there's a good reason to tell the same stories: While the stories never change, the readers do.

I've heard it said, "We do not tell stories as they are; we tell stories as we are." That seems right. The cells in our bodies are constantly dying and regenerating; new experiences are changing how we look at the world, and new friendships enrich how we walk through the world. And when the readers change, the stories change, too. The philosopher Heraclitus said we never stand in the same river twice. We also never stand in the same story twice. The stories we tell never stop speaking, creating new worlds.

In divinity school, I worked at a youth development program as a chaplain intern. It was the kind of work that was perfect for a theology student. You think you understand ontology until a fifteen-year-old asks who had sex to make God. If you could stumble through their questions, you could pastor a church and field most questions from the elderly women at the quilting club.

My group consisted of six thirteen- to eighteen-year-olds who had already experienced more hardship than most do in a lifetime. We gathered in a back room in the cottage, sharing the elements of Zebra Cakes and juice boxes.

We told stories.

"It wasn't the best decision," one story began. "The UPS driver left the keys in the ignition. It was around Christmastime, and I knew the truck would be full of things I wanted. Things I could resell. Things that could help my family get by. I got in the truck, even though I knew I shouldn't, and I drove the truck into the woods and began to unload it."

Or this one: "We used to leave the windows cracked at the motel so that we could sneak in and out. Gave us a place to sleep."

Most nights, we also read a story out of the Scriptures—a rendezvous between the stories of our lives and the stories of God and God's people. Occasionally, the collision would stir up a fight. Other times, we'd all get a breath of fresh air.

ANCIENT EXTRAVAGANCE

I'm not sure we can fully understand the Scriptures unless we occasionally read them behind bars. That shouldn't be surprising. Much of Scripture was written in jail cells or by people who spent some time there. Many of the earliest followers knew that if they followed Christ, they'd follow him right into a jail cell. Some of our top theologians did their best work in prison. Dietrich Bonhoeffer wrote in prison in Nazi Germany; Martin Luther King Jr. in a jail cell in Birmingham. God talks a little louder when faith is hard and suffering is immense.

One night, we read the story of the rich young ruler, more commonly known as the story of the wealthy White American's worst nightmare. You might remember this story, where Jesus asked the young man to give up everything and follow him. And the rich young ruler walked away heartbroken, for he had many possessions.

It's a hard story.

No. It's a hard story—for some.

It depends on who is in the room.

The boys in my group apparently thought this story was great news. Having given up everything, they had nothing left to lose. There was nothing in their hands to keep them from grabbing God's hand. The rest of us, meanwhile, are holding on tightly to the things we think will save us.

"What if God wants the poor to feel some of what that man is feelin' with his money?" one of the boys said.

The text never means only one thing. I thought the story was law, an indictment on our living. These boys thought the text was grace, a gift of liberation from God. I suppose it all depends on where you are standing. If you're standing up front, then you're bound to be last. But if you are last, then you might just be first.

◆

Rabbis used to say that there are "seventy faces of the Torah,"[5] indicating the richness of the text. "Turn it around and around, for everything is in it."[6] Stories are multivalent, with more meaning than we could ever grasp. You don't need a time machine to travel back to the first century to understand God. In that case, where you read Scripture is at least as important as where it was written. It's often more important. All interpretation is contextual—stories are written amid particular sociohistorical locations, but they encounter us in real, particular communities. It's a testament to a God who doesn't just speak in the past once and for all but an extravagant God who continually speaks in the present.

There is no final read of the story because the narrative is inevitably recast through the work of the Holy Spirit. "Who is Jesus for us today?" Dietrich Bonhoeffer frequently asked. A story is told repeatedly but never exhausted as it lives in the present context, shaping imaginations. The Bible ought to be read in the present tense as much as the past tense, if not more often. And we argue over the text until we discover God's message for us today—in this moment, in this place, with these people.

Some of the stories we were told as children were bad readings of the book. If so, we can try to tell a better one. A friend and mentee of mine just got ordained in the church. My best advice? Carry the stories of all those who went before you. Then, tell a better story, sing a more beautiful song, and share even better news. Go ahead and read the story. Turn it. Read it again.

There's a Jewish parable that speaks of a heated debate taking place in a park between two old and learned rabbis. The conversation in question revolves around a particularly complex and obscure verse in the Torah. These opponents have debated the text for years, nuancing their interpretation but never agreeing.

God listens patiently for years until God begins to tire of the endless debate. Finally, God decides to visit the two men and tell them once and for all what the verse means. God reaches down, pulls the clouds apart, and begins to speak: "You have been debating this verse endlessly for years; I will now tell you what it means. . . ."

But before God can continue, the two rabbis look up and say, in a rare moment of unity, "Who are you to tell us what the verse means? You have given us the words; now leave us in peace to wrestle with them."

Touching the Gospel
Living the Story

"What is God like to you?" I love to ask people. "Do you have a story about that?" One person told me that God used to be like a warm quilt she'd throw over her body, but now they rarely talk. Another: The minister had an affair, and it feels like God did, too. Still another says that she's been divorced from God since her parents divorced and left the church. Many people have a story about God, and a story about heartache is never far behind. I often listen to stories of pain because I ask to hear stories about God.

One of the first lessons I learned as a pastor is that I couldn't fix anyone's suffering. Mine was a helpless profession. Others can prescribe medicine or take a scalpel to the disease. The most I could offer anyone was presence. I could share in another's suffering—hold one's deepest regrets about the past and hope for the future to cope in the present. Will she ever come back? How can I go on without him? Was it my fault? How can I make it through the day? A pill can take away the pain, but a hand to hold will ease the suffering.

It's hard to receive another person's pain. Most people would rather suffer personally than sit with another who is suffering. When my wife and

I revealed we were having trouble conceiving, a friend blurted out, "You should just adopt." I thought in return, "And you should find a new friend."

Looking back, I don't blame him as much as I used to. I've learned it's easier to hand someone a dollar bill than to invite them in for a meal. And it's easier to invite someone to church than to ask them a story about God. We are prone to fixing, solving, conquering. And suffering can't always be fixed, though it can always be heard. Those of us who will suffer (all of us) need someone to remind us that suffering will always be a part of our story, but it will not always define our story.

We can heal.

In the Buddhist tradition, there is a story of a woman who lost her only son. The woman wrapped the body in linen, wailing and screaming in grief. She began to look for anyone who could resuscitate her child. Finally, she came across an elder in the village who knew of a way to bring her son back to life. The elder told her that her son could be raised to life, but only under one condition: She had to receive a mustard seed from a house where no one residing had ever lost a family member. If she could find just one seed, her son would return to life.

The woman packed a backpack with a few provisions and started her journey—stopping from house to house, listening to stories of death and grief. One had recently lost a grandmother. Another's husband had died years ago. Another lost an uncle and an aunt. She listened to stories of lost cousins, parents, and pets. After a few days, she realized that there was no one who didn't suffer the loss of a loved one.

Somewhere along the way, something astounding happened: She began to feel peace. As she listened to the stories of the suffering of others and shared the story of her own, she gradually accepted the loss of her son.

The best medicine for our suffering is sharing our story with someone who won't try to fix, correct, advise, or save us. The remedy is tender eyes and attentive ears, a head that nods gently.

If God creates with story, it makes sense that God heals with story. The story God heals with is Jesus. One of the church fathers says God will heal what God assumes.[1] I think that's to say that God heals primarily through presence in human nature. God did not remain aloof, but God's Word took on flesh and came to life to share in the story of humankind—write a new page in the annals of our history. In speaking the Word into humanity, God starts to heal our humanity.

Does it help to know that God understands? Jesus was God with diaper rash. A God with scraped knees. Bullied on the playground. God occasionally had terrible breath. Stomach viruses. Indigestion. He wept. This was a God who took a first breath and a last breath. Jesus's whole ministry reveals a God who enters our pain. God didn't deliver some mighty blow to suffering but endured the same pain and weakness as we do on our deathbeds. He hungered in the desert, wept at the grave of his best friend, and suffered the agony of physical and psychological pain on the cross. He hung next to criminals, and with them, he experienced agony.

Doesn't God begin to save us when God enters into all the crucifixions surrounding us? We have not a high priest who is unable to sympathize with our weaknesses. God becomes the incarnate Word when we have no words.

C. S. Lewis said, "Friendship is born at that moment when one says to another: 'What! You too? I thought that no one but myself!'"[2] It's hard to find those people. The writer Anne Lamott says the most powerful sermon in the world is just two words: "Me too."

> Me too. When you're struggling, when you are hurting, wounded, limping, doubting, questioning, barely hanging on, moments away from relapse, and somebody can identify with you—someone knows the temptations that are at your door, somebody has felt the pain that you are feeling, when someone can look you in the eyes and say, "Me too," and they actually mean it—it can save you. When you aren't judged, or lectured, or looked down upon, but somebody demonstrates that they get it, that they know what it's like, that you aren't alone, that's "me too."[3]

Jesus is how God says those two words, "Me too." When we knock on God's door and ask whether God has suffered loss, God tells us the story of Jesus—followed by the story of every human being since the beginning of time.

ANCIENT EXTRAVAGANCE

Once, Jesus told a story about a sower who flung seeds everywhere—indiscriminately—as if he were worried there would be a bare spot on the ground. The seed landed on the hard ground, but the path was sun-baked—with no moisture, it couldn't open up for the seed. The birds came and whisked the seed away as food for their babies. Other seeds landed in the rocks and took root, but the soil was too shallow to sustain the plants. Still others were choked out by the patches of briars. I imagine other seeds found a square inch of soft, fertilized soil between two rocks and blossomed into wheat that fed the entire community.

This is the way Jesus approached storytelling. Jesus was not careful and calculating—nor was he worried about waste. Jesus threw seeds of grace, came out with a watering can and gardening gloves, and waited to see what might grow.

Pharisees, lawyers, tax collectors—whoever—came to Jesus and asked concrete questions like, "What must I do to inherit eternal life?" Jesus rarely told them to memorize five propositions in the Torah or read over a catechism of the faith. He often said, "Let me tell you a story." And suddenly, everyone was subjected to hearing this mystical Middle Eastern rabbi ramble on about wheat and weeds.

Maybe something would grow. Often, it didn't. The surface was too dense. Cynicism, like a patch of briars, choked out the good news. Most of the time, his listeners walked away confused, angry and short-changed. But every once in a while, the seeds blossomed into a new creation.

The stories Jesus told are called parables, which are short stories that draw from local customs to say something about who we are, what's important, and how we might make sense of the world. The Greek root is *paraballō*, which means to throw alongside. In other words, Jesus met his listeners contextually by throwing down wisdom about God and God's kingdom alongside dining tables and banquets. Life's most ordinary, mundane objects and tasks reveal something about the kingdom of God.

Jesus had a particular pedagogy in mind with these stories—and it wasn't to answer questions. Socrates believed the teacher is like a midwife who helps the student give birth to the truth that resides within. Jesus, on the other hand, tells a story and confronts his disciples with something they could never discover for themselves. He tears down their world and then constructs a new one by talking about leaven, mustard seeds, or a journey from Jerusalem to Jericho. The listener must engage with the story and supply meaning and interpretation to the parable. And, if the hearer refuses to engage with Jesus about the interpretation of the story, then the message remains incomplete, laden with uncollected fruit. But if a person engages the story, then a person's whole world might be thrown off-balance.

The stories Jesus told aren't meant to function like a handbook—they're less about the information and more about the formation of a person. Jesus, through life and parable, disrupts and upends all our narcissistic ways of being in the world. Jesus pushes against the logic of domination that insists we can master God and God's Word by squeezing them into our preformed mental or philosophical or political constructs. We are invited into a narrative that conjures confusion, self-examination, greater self-awareness, and, perhaps, existential grappling. These stories give us the eyes to see ourselves and our world more clearly—warts, scars, and all. It hurts, but the pain wakes us from a fixed world where God's kingdom is too commonsensical.

"Seeing they do not perceive, and hearing they do not listen, nor do they understand" (Matt. 13:13).

There is, I think, a difference between wanting to possess the truth and wanting to be encountered by it. Most of us prefer the former, desiring the truth that fits our comfortable constructs and worldviews. Ideas are static and easy to control and mobilize. Social media, for instance, knows this and has an algorithm that only gives us what we want. The truth of a statement doesn't seem to matter as long as it insulates preconceived ideas or subdues another into our imagination of the world. It's the weaponization of facts. Here's what's worse: If we can intellectually master God, we can hold God at a distance instead of inviting the mystery and difficulty into our lives.

But God is not just a concept that must be grasped. God is a person waiting to be encountered. And that's why Jesus tells stories. Stories never stop speaking a new world into existence. Take this question: How should one describe a God who is profligate in grace and extravagant in pursuit of us? Here's a story:

> Which one of you, having a hundred sheep and losing one of them, does not leave the ninety-nine in the wilderness and go after the one that is lost until he finds it? And when he has found it, he lays it on his shoulders and rejoices. And when he comes home, he calls together his friends and neighbors, saying to them, "Rejoice with me, for I have found my lost sheep." (Luke 15:4-6)

This is not what I would do. But then again, I am not God. After all, the point of the story isn't to learn it but to become it.

• • • • • • • • • • • • • • • ✦ • • • • • • • • • • • • • • •

"They went out and fled from the tomb, for terror and amazement had seized them, and they said nothing to anyone, for they were afraid" (Mark 16:8).

Aristotle says a good story is one that you don't know how it will end, but you think it had to end that way when does end. Mark's ending of the resurrection story challenges that notion. It's the kind of ending that makes sense in a world of binging television series. The screen turns black, and the credits roll. The viewer clicks "next episode," and the series continues. In Mark's story, there is no upcoming episode. It's the series finale—*The Sopranos* of the Gospels. There is no Christ who is mistaken for the gardener, no Cleopas on the Emmaus Road, no doubting Thomas, no broiled fish by the fire.

Christ is risen!

They were afraid.

It's the kind of ending that makes sense for Mark, who gave us no birth story or angels. Jesus sprints toward the cross, rarely stopping for water.

But something seems missing. The story feels unfinished. We can imagine other endings—better endings. Maybe this is why monks started writing a bit of fan fiction to tell the story that the church deserves. In later editions of Mark, "Mark 2.0," Jesus appears to Mary Magdalene and commissions the disciples to tell the good news. Demons are cast out, and snakes will be handled. Jesus puts on his Wayfarers and ascends to the right hand of God.

If you look in the small print of your Bible, you will likely see that you have been given an opportunity to choose your own adventure. You can stop with the "shorter ending of Mark" or continue to the "longer ending" (and receive the chance to play with the snakes).

But that's not the story Mark tells. All the oldest and earliest manuscripts of Mark's Gospel end with a preposition, mid-sentence. The women and disciples were afraid, and they said nothing to anyone. Mark gives us the existentialist ending to the Gospel. There is no evidence that Jesus has, in fact, been risen. We only get a rumor from a kid dressed in white who is sitting on the right hand of the tomb.

"He ain't here," the kid says. "He'll meet you in Galilee."

It's possible that Mark knew the story had to end mid-sentence. Resurrection couldn't be the final word in God's story. Isn't it possible that resurrection was the first word of a new story? Contrary to popular expectations, Easter is not the ending. The story doesn't end until all things are made new.

And now Mark has given us the pen to help write a story we didn't start. We stand at a crossroads—do we follow Jesus to Galilee or return home and forget it ever happened?

I have chosen to gather up my fear, doubt, and faith and start walking to Galilee. There is no proof that he'll be there when I arrive. That's okay. It's a risk.

It's the next chapter of a great story.

Why not help write it?

Prodigal, Extravagant Love
Sharing the Story

One of my favorite of Jesus's stories is about two sons—one is wayward and the other is dependable (Luke 15:11–32). We call it the parable of the prodigal son, but Jesus never named his stories. It's not the name I would have chosen. Outside of this parable, we never use that word—prodigal: extravagantly wasteful, profligate, reckless. Oftentimes, we can just call these people Americans.

It's said that Charles Dickens called it "the greatest story ever told." Shakespeare used the language of this story as much as any other. Today, the tale of the wayward son is a standard Hollywood motif. The kid leaves, voyages, and sees the world. The boy comes back enlightened, humbled, and grateful. The parable even inspired one of the most recognizable hymns: "I once was lost, but now I'm found."

It's all amazing grace.

At the beginning of the story, a younger son asks his father (in the fashion of a youngest child) for his inheritance, something he would have received when his father died. This would have been surprising in light of all the clever and righteous younger sons throughout Scripture: Abel, Isaac, Jacob.

"Dad," he says. "It's time to hand over the '94 Nissan Sentra."

ANCIENT EXTRAVAGANCE

Some commentators say this is the same as telling his dad to die. There's no evidence for that, but there's plenty of evidence that this behavior breaks hearts. I dread the day that my child leaves town, visiting only over holidays and vacation. It doesn't take a sin to crush someone's heart.

The story goes that the kid travels to a faraway place. He explores foreign culture. He parties. He eats out of trash cans. All this happens until he starts working with pigs, an animal Jews were known to avoid. And he desires to eat what they are eating. He's starving. It's only then that he "wakes up to himself."

I used to attend a yearly retreat where the "prodigal" testimony was the highlight of the weekend. The speaker stood in the back of the dark sanctuary, a single candle flickering.

"There were drugs. And there were girls," he whispered.

"And then, I met Jesus."

Amazing grace.

"I was blind, but now I see."

Tears were shed. It's a foolproof structure.

This young prodigal son does what any starving youngest child would do: He calculates an apology that will make his father take him back as a hired hand. "I am no longer worthy to be called your son," he says. He goes home, not because he is sorry, but because he is hungry. And he trusts his father's goodness to take him back, especially if he sounds contrite.

There is a danger to recklessly pursuing—and forsaking everything else for—the immediate desires of one's own heart. So much of our youth is spent in thinking that happiness is found in ambition, success, the reckless pursuit of the things we hope will satisfy. And we're tempted to leave our relationships at the foot of the mountain as we climb toward self-fulfillment. It feels good until we realize the mountain keeps growing taller; there is no summit that will finally satiate our hearts. Liberation is found when we step off the mountain.

The older son, meanwhile, refuses to waste anything. He's stuck by his father's side and worked the family business—honored the family name (this is a story that refutes stereotypes, obviously).

One day the older brother is walking home from a long day working the fields. He's tired and hungry. And the house isn't quiet. There is music and dancing. Meat is being smoked on the grill. And then suddenly, he notices his little brother dressed in the finest clothes and jewelry. He's back from his soul-searching trip to India, being celebrated for squandering all of his inheritance.

The older son is furious.

He is, after all, the kind of person who played by all the rules. He worked hard, thought about retirement in his twenties, went to church at least once a week, volunteered at charities. He's kept his nose to the ground and never stepped out on a ledge to take a risk. Where's the party for him? We're taught that the world is a meritocracy. You reap what you sow. Where's the penance, the confession? His brother deserves a bottle of Aquafina, an apple from the yard, some hand-me-downs, and the night shift on the farm. But that's not what he gets.

The music is blaring, and the calf is on the grill. But the older son is off to the side, like a wallflower, watching, grumbling, and muttering under his breath. He's so offended by grace that he misses the party. He has lived a life of prodigal self-righteousness.

What's worse? The younger son is reckless in all the wrong places, but the older son refuses to be reckless at all.

⸻

Lastly, there is the father. And the father sees the son returning in the distance, stumbling down that dusty road. The father doesn't even wait for the son to ask for forgiveness when he shamelessly starts to run to meet him, embrace him, kiss him.

"Son, you once were dead, but now you've come to life. You once were lost, and now have been found." He throws the party of the century with wasteful extravagance—DJs, grass-fed beef, a robe made of the finest cashmere and silk, shoes lined with the finest wool.

He then approaches his older son, who believes he has earned what his father has given to him. The father says to this son, "You are always with me, and all that is mine is yours" (Luke 15:31). There is nothing more to give the older son, because he has already given him his whole heart.

· · · · · · · · · · · · · · · ◆ · · · · · · · · · · · · · · ·

Jesus begins the tale by saying, "There was a man who had two sons." The father is the subject, not the sons. And there's a hint to read Scripture well. It's always about the Father. It's not about the times you've stayed out too late at the bar. Or whether you've spent all your money searching for that elusive "something more." And it's not about your perfect attendance at church or how many times you've volunteered at the soup kitchen. You simply cannot earn the Father's care.

The Father? Why, he must be the most prodigal of them all. He has given his two sons everything, even after they've stomped on his heart. Not one ounce of love is withheld.

It turns out that this parable might be about the God of Israel. After all, that's the God who loves the Pharisees and the Gentiles. Younger and older. Sinner and saint. The extravagant love of God is poured out for the sinner who is also righteous. And the righteous who is also a sinner.

No matter who you are, Jesus's question is the same: Will you come to the party? God is longing for you to come home. Can you smell the calf? Do you hear the music?

The table has been set for you.

INTERLUDE

WASTED TIME

The Longest, Shortest Time

I was told the same adage repeatedly after my kids were born: "The longest, shortest time." You'll hate the sleepless nights, but pay attention, savor the moment, and don't take the newborn cuddles for granted. Blink and they'll be in college.

It's accurate. All of my wife's journal entries from the first three months read, "Will this ever end?" I tried blinking a number of times to speed through changing diaper blowouts. It didn't work. My youngest, who was possessed by a form of the demonic called "colic," could only be pacified when we bounced her on a yoga ball. We dreaded sunset and wished the time away.

Then we blinked, and they were babbling.

Blink.

Walking.

Blink.

Running and cursing.

A friend of mine told me that there will be a day when my daughter won't want to hold my hand. It was unnecessary commentary. Time is a series of deaths.

Blink.

We live our lives grasping tightly to both ends of the paradox—the longest, shortest time. On one hand, we live our lives like we're immortal—we're always guaranteed another day. When I leave work, I say, "See you tomorrow." We talk about time like it's a commodity under our control. We talk about spending and saving it like it's capital, or a piece of money. I need to find a way to buy some more time, we say, as if it's something we can purchase when it runs out. We talk about making time, as if we can smash a button on our watch and create more during an inordinately busy week. We quantify and externalize time, but a clock will only measure our location as we revolve around the sun.

Time is long, and therefore nothing is urgent. Most of us can point to a person who is completely satisfied with treading water in the shallow end of the pool. They spend their days livin' on a unicorn inflatable. Time is postponed to the future, and so the present is lost in the frivolous pursuits of the finite. There is an endless sea of methods to distract yourself from finitude, the reality that you, me, your dog, and even the squishy baby next door will pass away.

The Roman poet Juvenal says the Roman Empire promised two things to distract the people from their hardship: bread and circuses.[1] As it turns out, these are also great distractions from existential angst. We really only want food and entertainment. A full stomach and a good movie. Collegiate and professional sports are an effective way to spend an entire day distracting ourselves from the reality that we will work until we die. Minutes are absorbed by screens. We scroll through our lives as we touch our phones thousands of times across a few hours.

This is to say that we live distracted, moving from circus to circus. Do we realize that what we do matters? Has deep significance? Time ceases to be an invaluable gift when there is no urgency. We rob the world of our giftedness. Life must be lived.

Maybe it's more common to be all too cognizant of the time we have left. It's best to look our finitude in the face and live like there is no tomorrow. Samuel Johnson said, "When any man knows he is to be hanged in a fortnight, it concentrates his mind wonderfully."[2] Do we have the courage to look at the end without flinching? If we can, we might make the most of today.

They say we shouldn't waste our lives. I'm not sure who "they" are, but I know their message has been resounding in my head ever since I was a kid. "You only get one life" is one of the great American philosophies, and one of the reasons why I take Lexapro. More than likely, you're the kind of person who has digested this message, too.

I remember lying in my bed as a middle schooler calculating the percentage of time I had left. My grandfather died of early-onset Alzheimer's. I did the math. He died at sixty-four years old. If I was fifteen years old, then I had lived about one-fourth of my life. By the time I graduated college, one-third of my life would be over. Best to start having babies at eighteen to get them out of the house by thirty-six.

Time, then, is a scarce commodity that you need to ration efficiently. You'll grow older before you like, and no amount of wrinkle cream will convince me otherwise. You will absorb time and wear its effects on your body. Your hair will turn gray, and the hairline will recede. Betrayed by your body, you'll start feeling pain when you jog. Then when you stand up. Finally, when you sleep. You'll buy another handheld massager for your back.

Time makes its way into your inner life. Your brain, the time capsule of your life, will take longer to process its contents. When you're young, information happily travels from one place to the next. It moves slower as you age. A neuron dies. So does a memory. There's a roadblock on a neural pathway. People and places disappear as if they never existed.

Meanwhile, your babies will become toddlers, and youth, and adults. They'll have kids of their own. You'll wonder if you've wasted too much time.

· · · · · · · · · · · · · · · ✦ · · · · · · · · · · · · · · ·

Doesn't it feel like time is speeding up? One sociologist, Hartmut Rosa, talks about the disease of acceleration.[3] The world is speeding up and it's not just a figment of our imagination. It's not that we've entered the twilight zone and the planets are somehow revolving around the sun at a faster speed. Instead, our lives are revolving around technology and social change at light speed. There is never enough time to accomplish what needs to be done. To maintain the status quo of our lives, technological acceleration and cultural innovation are necessary.

ANCIENT EXTRAVAGANCE

Here's a fictitious illustration that's likely not at all fictitious: You wake up to your phone beeping, check your digital mail, send a handful of personal letters that are delivered immediately from the comfort of your mattress. Then, you jump in a car, a plane, and an Uber and arrive halfway across the country. It's only three o'clock p.m. and you've arrived just in time for whatever meeting is on the docket for the day. When the meeting is over, you still have more time to send out a few letters before you call it a day. There, you've accomplished a week's amount of work in less than twenty-four hours.

I noticed this acutely in my life while watching television. Yes, television. Television, once immune to acceleration, was the one lifeline you had to escape the hardships of your life (bread and circuses, remember?). In the nineties, you could count on the box to give you a mediocre program that would entertain you without demanding anything in response. There was no wrong programming choice because there was often no good choice. It was our last bastion of grace. Now we live in a world with Netflix, Hulu, Amazon Prime, and HBO Max. You can't keep up with all of it and still work and eat and breathe and have a social life. Worse yet, a lot of it is actually good. A new show is released every week and it's certified fresh, or a must-watch prestige program. Not only that, many of us are also likely to get on Reddit fan boards and fire up a podcast to fully comprehend the plot, camera movements, and directorial decisions.

Do you feel the pressure to get it all in?

Your social life is speeding up, too. You can't keep up in the office banter if you haven't fired up Spotify, looked at the latest [insert sport] statistics, and kept an eye on the latest political blunder. The words you said last year are no longer hip or trendy; they're offensive. Our social norms have jumped on a bullet train, but many of us are stuck in the eighties. When did we stop writing "guys" and start writing "folx"? And what's the *x* for, anyway? Okay, boomer. You're outdated. Stop quoting movies from the nineties. But I'm a millennial!

Time is speeding up, and we are restless—literally unable to rest.

All these advances and time-saving devices are meant to ease the burden of living. We have machines to cook our food in under a minute so that we'll have more time to sit leisurely around the table creating relationships. But that's not what happens. We still have the same amount of time units, but we can increasingly accomplish double and triple the amount of work in each unit—simultaneously having digital meetings with people all over the country while sending letters that are delivered immediately.[4] You've saved time—for more work. You're running faster, but you're on a hamster wheel, locked inside of a cage. It's isolating you from everything you hold most dear.

This is all to say that the best way we know how to deal with the deficit of time is by filling it—every hour. When the hours are full, fill the minutes. We've become modern-day Stoics: "Live each day as if it were your last." Do not be afraid to die; be afraid to never have truly lived. When you die, your gravestone will have two dates and a dash in between. How much did you fit into the dash? Fill that dash to the brim. When it's full, keep pouring more in. You can paraphrase all of this by saying "YOLO," or "you only live once." It's the new way of saying "carpe diem," seize the day.

For many of us, busyness is the best philosophy of time that we've got. This is the American way: If we can do something, we must do something.

This afternoon, I was leisurely sitting at a coffee shop when a ministry acquaintance showed up and sat down beside me. "What are you up to?" he asked. The problem was that I had an empty calendar. And I—who was not doing much of anything—fabricated a whole agenda of items that I was (not) doing: preparing to teach a class, checking up on a mentee, solving the housing crisis in Atlanta, making sure the world is still spinning. If you're not busy, then it's best to pretend you are, lest someone presumes something is wrong with you.

"What are you doing?" I asked in return.

Oh, you only have a meeting.

Must be nice to have a light day.

It's hard to be a loser, to accomplish nothing, to sit at the coffee shop for two hours and read. Busy people are important people. I need busyness around to constantly reassure me and tell me I'm important. She tells me that I'm making a difference. I'm indispensable. She will save me, give my life meaning, create resources for my safety. She's the most important priority in my life. Busyness is a god.

This approach to time isn't just unhealthy; it's a disease. "I confess to you, Lord, that I still do not know what time is," Augustine admitted, "and I further confess to you, Lord, that as I say this, I know myself to be conditioned by time."[5] Germans, who develop the best words for almost everything, have a diagnosis: Zeitkrankheit. It's "time sickness" or "hurry sickness." Many of us suffer from the sickness of time.

We need a new way of telling time. Or maybe we ought to pray the prayer of the psalmist: "Teach us to count our days that we may gain a wise heart" (Ps. 90:12).

Evening, Morning—A Day

Every clock or calendar is a way of organizing time. But it's all artificial. Time is an unquantifiable thing that we try to quantify. You've managed your time well, but what time is it? Hours can fall back and spring forward. A month can leap. Must a year follow the solar cycle, marked by equinoxes and solstices? And how should we measure a day? Does a day start at sundown? In the middle of the night? Or when the sun rises?

In the beginning, God numbered our days and filled them with meaning through the creation of the Earth. It's our first lesson in telling time. The repetition and rhythm of the creation poem mirror our lives. Birds chirp, and the coyotes yelp. We plow, we plant, we harvest. The beats are the same every day, but God plays a new song. The Earth turns on its axis and revolves around the sun, and God gives us the basic two-beat rhythm of life: evening and morning—a new day.

Did you notice that human life begins with rest in Scripture?

How odd.

God animates a lump of dirt with divine breath late on the sixth day and tells it to rest on the seventh. The divine dirt clod hasn't even done anything before laying down its head, pulling the eye mask over its face, and enjoying a deep sleep. The wisdom of creation is the priority of rest.

I think this is why the rhythm of evening, morning is the basic pattern for the Hebrew day. In the Hebrew clock, the sound of a wine bottle being uncorked in the evening is the alarm that awakens you to a new day. You make your bed with the moon before you rise with the sun. Busyness might arrive later in the day, but only if time permits. There is being before doing and death before life.

In other words, there is evening, there is morning—a new day.

◆

This philosophy of time makes no sense for most Christians in the United States. For us, the new day officially begins in the middle of the night when everyone but young adults and infants and their parents are asleep. But in the popular imagination, the new day starts with sunlight breaking through the curtain. The day begins with restlessness. The beeping of the alarm clock stops your heart, jolts you to life, and you roll out of bed. Shower, brush, change. You might have time to drink a cup of coffee in your favorite reading chair (that depends on whether you have children and whether you stayed up too late binging some overrated TV show). Go ahead and pour the coffee into a cheap travel mug. It will taste like aluminum, but you will get to work on time. And the countdown begins: There are twelve hours until you've earned time to rest.

There's nothing more American than believing we earn our rest. Rest, if there is any to be had, is a reward for spending at least eight hours toiling in the sun or staring at a computer with horrible back posture (you really ought to grunt when you lengthen your spine at the end of the day). Rest is governed by meritocracy—we earn vacation. Sick time is a luxury you receive once you've been at the job for a few months. Women go into labor, pushing new life into the world through blood and pain; they earn one month to recover. The meritocracy of rest infiltrates the rhythm of my normal day. I allow myself one hour of rest, and one hour only, once the kids are snoring and the email inbox has been cleared.

There is morning, there is evening—a new day.

According to the creation story, though, rest isn't a reward for labor but a fundamental gift for humanity. Eugene Peterson notes that the creation story reminds us that God always goes before us, preveniently, in grace—even in creation.[1] The pattern for all life is that we must receive before we offer. Even an apple tree will receive care for five to ten years before it bears fruit. That means it's totally permissible to rest your body for sixteen hours before you spend the next eight working.

Our frantic activity (errands and email and school pickup lines and meetings and grocery shopping) begins halfway through the day. But the day is already half past! That's right, and God has managed without us just fine. When we open our eyes for the first or ten millionth time, we awake to a God who has already been on the scene. God has been working all night, tending to all that is growing. Then we are called to respond to God's work by picking up our tools and watering cans.

We're more dispensable than we think. Every time we close our eyes, the world takes care of itself. We lie unconscious for six, eight, ten hours, and the sun still rises without our prompting. I know you were taught to believe you are the main character of the film—that the plot would go to hell if you vanished for a day or two. Who will carry the conversation? Keep the audience laughing? Tie the loose ends and bring the drama to its logical conclusion?

You're important, but the show will go on without you.

It's a blow to our egos. But if you have ever left a job position that you truly loved, you will know this is true. You might get on social media, expecting that your former place of employment went up in flames without you. This is rarely the case. More often, time marches on (more or less) as normal. Your former boss is still inept, and the person who replaced you hasn't made any significant changes. They're still in debt. We ought not to be surprised; the earth was turning long before we arrived and will likely turn long after we're gone.

The limit is grace—a taste of freedom. It's not on your business card to ensure the world keeps turning, after all. And the most fundamental part of your humanity is not work but delight.

The first thing on your calendar is rest. Your work, if it must be done, ought to be scheduled after you spend time in delight. And that's how we are taught to mark a day: There is evening, morning—the first day.

A Moment of Silence

Be still and know I Am God.

Be still and know I Am

Be still and know

Be still

Be

A Week

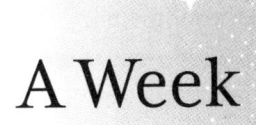

While evening and morning give us the right rhythm of the day, the week's design commemorates the creation of the earth with Sabbath (shabbat) arriving on the seventh day. The Sabbath, which literally means "quit" or "stop" or "take a break," is the first lesson we received about what it means to be a human being. In the creation story, humanity first opens its eyes, rubs the crust from its eyelids, and sees a God walking through the garden. There was plenty to do, but God wasn't fertilizing or pruning. Rest was not just the first activity of humankind.

Rest was also their first experience of God.

What kind of God rests? Again, a God who is not anxious, which means a God who is not American. Perhaps this is a God who will read a book in a hammock, or a God of art museums and symphonies. A God who enjoys long, drawn-out meals. In the way the creation poem reads, I imagine the seventh day as a dinner party. God has prepared the food, set the table, and waits for the world to dine. Sabbath is the conversation, laughter, wine, and post-meal naps. There is enough food. God won't let the cup run dry. Creation's wellness does not depend on endless work.

I think the point is this: If God can knock off for a day after creating the universe, then you could probably do the same thing after your nine-to-five. Stop. And in the stopping, delight. And in the delighting, become human.

ANCIENT EXTRAVAGANCE

I don't presume that most of us know what it means to delight anymore. Many of us are so efficient and calculated and productive and important and busy that we've forgotten what it means to delight. You might have to dig deep into the recesses of your memory and find those moments when urgency exchanged places with wonder and playfulness. Delight is the moments when you feel most connected to others, or the ground, or your own self. Time changes.

Have you ever woken up, peered out the window, and been surprised by a blanket of snow covering the ground? If you grew up in the Deep South or far north, let me explain what happens in temperate climates. The weather people have informed you that there's a 70 percent chance of rest (or snow) before you put your head down to sleep. This means there will be one-eighth of an inch or a snow-pocalypse. There is no in-between. You fall asleep hoping—praying—begging that God will drop the temperature just two more degrees. In the morning, you rush to the window to look outside. The local news confirms your suspicion: no school.

If you're an adult, you call out of work, including virtual work. Best not to take a chance on the black ice, you say. Anyway, the meeting is not likely to be more important than staring out the window with a cup of hot chocolate. The world moves slow enough to notice ice crystals falling from the sky. With nowhere to go, nothing to do, you unwrap rest while all the critters slowly get out of bed. The streets shut down and everything is quiet, until the silence is finally broken by crunching snow beneath your feet. It's an open invitation to be a child again—binge those classics and make a snowman.

Make a snow-family.

It's a complete waste of time. And that's the point.

My other favorite moments of delight took place after the birth of each of my children. There was nothing like it. Even vacations have to-do lists—things to see and meals to plan. But child leave, if you're lucky to get it, is mostly empty. It might last a week, or a month—six months if you're lucky. Time will soon march on with even more noise. But first, there is emptiness. Eyes are closed on and off throughout the day. No one is talking about the debt ceiling or the latest missile. No toil. Microsoft Calendar reminders are snoozed. Snacking replaces three structured meals. Coffee hour is any hour. Your best friends will stop by with meals, hoping to squeeze chunky, soft newborn skin.

After the birth of our second, my wife glanced over to me on the couch and said, "What day is it?" Light and dark were intertwined. My only concern was the wiggly cherub in my lap. Do we have enough diapers? Is he feeding enough? Why is this meconium so hard to scrub off his bottom? Stress melted away as we held beauty incarnate.

I then understood why God created Sabbath after the birth of God's children. These moments felt different than a day off—they were an interruption, or a disruption, to time. Time was fundamentally changed.

James K. A. Smith notes that we too often ask ourselves "Where am I?" but the more constructive question is "When am I?"[1] We must attend to ourselves in time to know who we are and how to behave. If we are always somewhere, then it's equally true that we are always sometime.

When are we?

God is not always found in the right places so much as in the right times. Abraham Heschel insists that God is concerned with making holy time rather than holy places. Heschel observes that God ended each day of creation by calling it "good," but when God created the seventh day, or the Sabbath day, God called it "holy." Here's how Heschel puts it: "Six days a week we live under the tyranny of things of space; on the Sabbath we try to become attuned to *holiness in time*. It is a day on which we are called upon to share in what is eternal in time, to turn from the results of creation to the mystery of creation; from the world of creation to the creation of the world."[2] Sabbath is an altar in time rather than place.

In Scripture, holiness means to be set apart in mind, action, speech, and character. It's a polite way of saying you should be a little weird. You might be on the right track toward holiness if someone says to you, "Well, that's a strange way to live your life." To which you will reply, "Thank you."

Goodness and holiness are not synonymous. I know this is confusing because good people are often ridiculed as holy people (*ehem* Holy

Rollers). But one can be good and not be holy. Or maybe it's the case that everyone is fundamentally good by virtue of creation, but not everyone and everything is holy, or set apart. And the holiness, when practiced well, is meant to remind the world of its goodness.

Here's another way to think about it: A day off is good, but it's not always holy. Alternatively, the Sabbath, when kept faithfully, is always holy. Eugene Peterson says that a "day off" is a bastard Sabbath.[3] Oftentimes, a day off is a gift from capitalism and not God—the day you watch enough football and drink enough beer to get through another week. With capitalism, rest is driven by economics and the need to work harder the rest of the week (these are the people who tell you to rest well so you're sure to work harder the next day). If you're resting to recover from the previous week, or to prepare for the week to come, then you're not practicing Sabbath.

Sabbath, on the other hand, is holy. An end in itself. You stop. Breathe. And likely, you'll realize you haven't done either of those things over the last six days. In stopping and breathing, your rest refuses metrics of efficiency. You are mindful of time's depth, reinvigorated by the world's goodness. And in the process, you become a person set apart, different from the rest of the world.

In Greek, the language of the New Testament, there are two words for time: *kairos* and *chronos*. *Chronos* is the root of our word "chronological." It's the sequence of moments that are measured by the watch on your arm or the clock on your phone. Chronos is time measured by appointments, meetings, and events for which you have to arrive on time. Generally speaking, chronos is stressful.

But the other word is *kairos*. And kairos is not about length, but depth. Kairos is the "right time," the "good opportunity," the "unique chance." In kairos time, "Everything has its time." These are the moments you say, "I wish I could make this moment last forever." It's holy time—set apart.

Kairos is the first loud cry and the last quiet exhale. The moment after the first sip of coffee before the first kid climbs out of bed asking for a drink. It's a dinner table with friends (with one too many IPAs). Kairos is the belief that every moment is pregnant with eternity. Paul Tillich said kairos means that every moment might be the small gate through which the Messiah will enter.[4] You don't necessarily need more moments to meet the Messiah; you just have to pay attention to the moments you've got.

Sabbath is not another entry in the sequence of events on the calendar; it's the kairotic moment when God squeezes through the gate of the finite. Søren Kierkegaard says one moment (Øieblikket) has the possibility to change everything. Take Jesus, for instance. In Jesus, the eternal has entered the temporal—in a moment. When the eternal made an appearance in time, our clocks stopped working. "All eternity is in the moment," says Mary Oliver.[5] Every moment is infinitely momentous. In the blink of an eye, you can be absorbed into the eternal, plunged to the depths of the sea, or raised above the heavens.

Be present in every moment, because your life may change forever in just one instant.

We make a mistake when we say that Sabbath is about time management; Sabbath is about the reconstruction of time. It's the sanctification of time, or the way that our time becomes shaped by kairos (holiness) rather than chronos (length). In Sabbath time, there's time to waste, because wasted time can be the holiest time of all. You can enjoy a sunset and waste a night with friends around the dinner table. Dance. Sit with a friend, get lost on a walk, or welcome the stranger for a cup of tea. There's time to feed the hungry or to paint a landscape. Cry. Sing a song or wash someone's feet.

These wasted and holy moments are not supposed to be an interlude, or the exception to our time, but time as it is meant to be experienced.

--- ✦ ---

Recently, I was sitting at a brewery with some friends of a friend who were talking about gaming. "You must not play," they said.

Nope.

"You look like a golfer. Do you golf?" I was wearing skinny jeans and a Patagonia hat. Obviously, the only golf ball I've ever hit was sprayed with adhesive glue, lit on fire, and smacked into a lake.

"Well, what do you do?" one asked, as if gaming and golf are the only two hobbies for White men in their 30s (he forgot about football, IPAs, and smoking meat).

I sat in silence until my friend said, "You're into music. We connect over that."

"Yeah, that's right. Music," I replied.

Kind of.

Have you ever had a moment when you realized you have no idea how to practice delight? It's a polar plunge for your soul. I do a little of a lot of things, but most of the things I do are connected to work. I read. I write. I think—hard—and read and write some more. I watch certified-fresh television. I am quite adept at taking activities that are meant for pleasure and using them for work. I run, for instance, but only because I have high cholesterol. It just so happens that running also creates an opening in time to think about reading and writing. I shun the Sabbath.

A former teacher of mine coined the "Sabbath paradox": Sabbath is the most desperately needed and least followed practice.[6] We long for rest and rejuvenation, but we fail to take it when it's given. And we're stripped of our humanity, enslaved to the machine that demands ceaseless work and productivity.

I'm not at all surprised that Sabbath keeping was incorporated into God's top ten commandments for the Hebrew people. It's one of two Ten Commandments I break regularly (the other is taking the Lord's name in vain). The other nine besides Sabbath are serious—murder, stealing, and covetous rage. Break one of these nine and there are going to be consequences. What's the consequence for breaking Sabbath? A promotion? A cleaner house?

I feel no remorse for breaking the Sabbath. In fact, resting bestows a greater guilt. This, alone, is proof that my conscience is shaped by the virtues of the market: efficiency, production, impatience, competition. I wonder if this is why the Sabbath commandment is the longest commandment of the ten, taking up about one-third of all the words. Length doesn't always equate with significance, but God might know we need the extra words to be convinced to take it seriously.

When Moses recounts the presentation of the law, he offers a different reason for Sabbath: justice. In the story of the exodus, we are told that Pharaoh suffered anxious night terrors of famine and scarcity. The Israelites worked, therefore, so Pharaoh could rest. They laid bricks, sweating in the hot sun, so that Pharaoh could create more "supply cities" in his endless accumulation of wealth. Slavery was a symptom of the anxiety of the powerful; those at the bottom of the pyramid of life lay their bricks so that the few at the top can get a good night's rest.

The commandment to rest is a gift that challenges an economy of restless striving. Moses puts it this way: Remember when you were enslaved by Pharaoh in Egypt and you worked seven days a week? And Pharaoh defined you by the number of bricks you laid while you were sweating in the sun? There was no time for rest. Now, you observe rest as a matter of justice (Deut. 5:12–15). You have been freed from slavery. When you stop, you acknowledge that the world doesn't belong to you. You live in God's world. And God's world operates not with scarcity but with abundance.

Pharaoh lives and breathes today, demanding our own restless striving for accumulation. Like Pharaoh, our own scarcity mentality leads us to fill storage units to create a fragile sense of control over our own mini kingdoms. But hoarding resources only offers a fleeting reprieve from the relentless demands of our restlessness.

During the week, we are enslaved by our work, our appointments, our extracurriculars. We are told when to arrive and when to leave. We are told when to eat. That new hobby is a perfect side hustle. Monetize it. The phones in our pockets function like an extra appendage. Work is now a part of our bodies—always accessible. We can check our email while we're out to dinner with loved ones. We can listen to a lecture while our kids play soccer. We can do it all.

That's Pharaoh whispering to you. It's the same voice that tempted Jesus in the wilderness—to have more, be more, and live without limits. Temptation is crafty because it doesn't come from a little man in a red suit. If it did, it would be much easier to refuse. More often, evil sounds like our own voice: "You can have more." Enslaved to consumption, we turn stones into bread and satiate our every want. Enslaved to power, we come in early and stay a few hours late to climb to the top of the mountain. Enslaved to success, we throw ourselves at the feet of the powerful so we can be seen.

We never stop.

The god of work is one of the lousiest of the idols. It smiles like the serpent in the garden and tells us that we can live without limits. And then it demands we sacrifice our humanity on the altar of production. We give away our relationships and lose our connection to the material world. We dip our fingers into our bank account to remember who we are. It's an empty promise. We won't become like God, because even God knows how to rest. Instead, we become enslaved to time. We have given our entire lives to a pyramid scheme.

Moses reminds us: "Do you, when you wake up in the night, remember what you were supposed to have done, vexed that you did not meet expectations? Do you fall asleep counting bricks? Do you dream of more bricks you have to make yet, or of bricks you have made that were flawed? We dream so because we have forgotten the exodus!"[7]

Put the work away. Give the middle finger to Pharaoh and reclaim your identity. Your work doesn't define you. It never did. No one really cares about your title or your degrees. Your '03 Honda runs just fine. And you certainly don't want your children to end up living like you.

That's why God commands Sabbath. Every Sabbath is a mini exodus when you cross through the Red Sea into freedom. In the promised land, clocks don't move according to the same speed. In keeping Sabbath, we cast our vote for a new economy.

Sabbath isn't just rest.

It's justice.

◆

Easy for you to say, you might be thinking. I know all this seems hopelessly romantic—that you can save your life by going on more walks. It seems like every year a new book on busyness lands on *The New Times* bestseller list armed with new strategies to defeat hurriedness, be more present, and have more dinner parties.

Did you know that the key to changing your life is a pilgrimage to India?

No one becomes less busy by reading a book by wealthy, accomplished people. Curiously, the best strategy to defeat busyness is to have money. Go on a date night, they say. How brave! And expensive (I'm talking childcare, here). You can spend your way to a healthier, slower life by hiring babysitters or by paying someone to do your laundry and mop your floors. It's less courageous to take a demotion at work when you don't need the cash to feed your family. By the way, more dinner parties won't save your life when you get off work at six o'clock.

The decision to move slower is a Band-Aid on a gaping wound on a society that needs reconstructive surgery. Most people are at the mercy of the economy. Busyness is the ocean we swim in, and we have no power to get out of that water completely. The best we can do is try to change the temperature.

That's why Scripture's take on time isn't individualistic. Sabbath is a communal practice. There's one more step, then, to wasting time, and it might be the most important of all of them: Share the wastefulness.

There is a corporate nature to our rest. Walter Brueggemann says the odd insistence of the God of Sinai is to counter anxious productivity with committed neighborliness.[8] In other words, we counter the anxiety of individual ambition with communal care. We are all one domino in a long line of dominoes. When you receive an exodus from your work, you also release others from the work that binds them. Cease all forms of domination, lest you become Pharaoh yourself.

In the Scriptures, the Sabbath commandment is not just for you but also for everyone above you and below you and below them. Rest is particularly important for those who don't have voices to advocate for their own delight. It's for your son and your daughter, but also your slave and your livestock. It's for the immigrant who is waiting for work outside of the Home Depot. Even the land ought to rest—the lily in the field and the apple tree on the farm.

You might think you don't have any power to give another rest, but that's likely not the case. Start with the most obvious: any people you supervise. They are worthy of freedom—the occasional short day, reasonable health and family leave, flexible hours when possible. You might have children, too, who get home from school exhausted from a day of learning. But then you have scheduled them to go to piano and soccer and art club. Oh yeah, they also have homework that is too advanced for them to do on their own.

You've just become the family's pharaoh.

Maybe none of this rings true, but you have a little patch of land that you can let rest by refusing to pump it full of artificial nitrogen so that it can work harder. Your vines and trees might even repay you with more and richer produce; but even if they don't, you've honored their sanctity. Or you might have no land whatsoever, but you can choose to buy fruits and vegetables, meat and poultry, from land that was given the opportunity to rest. Every purchase is a vote for the world we want to inhabit.

Most days this way of living will feel wasteful. You likely won't overthrow an economic system or change an entire culture of busyness. That's okay. You'll be free. While Pharaoh anxiously accumulates wealth, you will resist with porches and picnic blankets. More still, Pharaoh will be excommunicated from your heart and the hearts you hold dear. In Pharaoh's place, God will enter with a lawn chair and a margarita.

※※※※※※※※※※※※※ ✦ ※※※※※※※※※※※※※

Sabbath, then, is about the micro-practices of resistance. They might be small, but we're part of a tradition that knows a slingshot can slay Goliath. In a fourteenth century text, *The Cloud of Unknowing*, an unnamed English monk writes, "You only need a tiny scrap of time to move toward God."[9] All it takes is a shred of the day.

I rarely attain a full day of Sabbath. I'm not even sure how to begin to imagine a day, consisting of twenty-four long hours, fashioned in delight. You, too, might feel intimidated by the prospects of an empty day. I once heard of a church that offered each parishioner a shot of vodka at the conclusion of the Sunday worship service. I'm not advocating for road beers on the way home from church, but sometimes it takes a little liquid to find the courage to rest.

Maybe we ought to start small. The first move is to choose the right day. Sabbath doesn't have to take place on Sunday. In fact, Sunday might be a poor choice. Churches are great at infusing their festal day of rest with work. Not only do you have to get up, drive to worship, and make conversation with friends and strangers, but you'll likely be asked to volunteer at the food pantry or the children's nursery. These are good deeds, but they're also work. Today, my daughter woke up and asked if we still had worship in the summer. Worship can be work during the season of our rest.

When you look closely, there is no mention of attending organized worship on Sabbath in the Scriptures. Prior to the rule of Constantine, the early church kept Sabbath from sundown on Friday to sundown on Saturday. They were Jewish people, and Sabbath was kept the day before the day of worship. Let's not be sticklers, returning to a world with blue laws and draconian restrictions. You can keep Sabbath on Saturday rather than Sunday, if you'd like. Tuesday is a natural choice if you work the weekends. It's the introvert of the week. I've never met a Tuesday that clamored for my attention. Again, this is all up to you.

Have you learned how to say no? It's another micro-practice of resistance. Learning to say no and yes to the right things is a habit that requires careful attention. Anne Lamott says, "Almost everything will work again if you unplug it for a few minutes, including you."[10] I've found this to be true. You've got to unplug the console, take out the cartridge, shake it, and blow in it just a little bit before you reinsert it. Younger generations know that when the app freezes, you have to swipe it up into outer space, exit, and reboot. I can't manage two hard runs on consecutive days, and my brain is fried after four uninterrupted hours of hard writing. When I go to the doctor complaining about my lethargy, she asks: Are you powering down and getting enough rest?

Those of us who were raised to not disappoint will have a hard time with this. Tim Ferriss, a self-help guru, offers advice that is generally helpful: If it's not a "hell yes," then it's gonna be a no. What good things do we need to say no to? Another piece of advice is to imagine that the opportunity would be on the calendar tomorrow instead of its original date. Would you dread going? If you would dread going tomorrow, then you'll likely dread it two months down the road.

It's easy to get caught up debating about what "counts" as work on the Sabbath, which is why our forebears have created all kinds of lists and prohibitions. Rabbis have spent all kinds of time trying to classify prohibitions to sanctify the Sabbath: Don't drive, don't cook, don't turn on electricity. In the United States, there are still plenty of counties that prohibit the sale of alcohol on Sundays—or until noon on Sunday. The letter of the law obscures the spirit. Let's be honest, you are the best judge of the kind of work that sucks your soul dry and zaps the joy right out of your life. Say no. Do it for yourself, your family, your culture and economy, your church. We'll all reap the benefits.

Here's the point: When we learn to say no, we replant the Tree of Knowledge of Good and Evil in the middle of the garden and build a nice fence around it. The world is not ours, and we don't have to pick fruit from every tree.

Once you learn to say no to the right things, you might take up the practice of saying yes. Rest, in the Scriptures, is an action (*menuha*). That's to say, it's something you do rather than something you passively receive when you've used up all your energy and have nothing left to offer the world and pass out on the couch. This must be why Sabbath keeping consists of the decisions we make as much as the ones we don't.

It's okay to start with small choices—with coffee, for instance. Buy the beans from companies that don't make profit by enslaving land and human beings. Grind them because there is time to waste. Pour it in your favorite coffee mug. I know that it only holds seven ounces, but it feels good in your hands. It's okay to get up and refill it in fifteen minutes.

There, you've made your first series of moments holy.

Some activities become richer when we do them with less efficiency. Pen pals are nice. Write a letter and feel the tip of the pencil rub against the grain of the paper. Write each letter slowly, paying attention to the love that's being infused in the charcoal. Spend time with the youngest and the oldest in our society. Christians are the kind of people who have time for the people who can't repay us (except, maybe, with wisdom).

Chop an onion—slowly. I know that it's tempting to get through an onion as fast as possible, lest you cry or your fingers absorb its oil. An onion is not just a means to tastier food. It is its own magnificent piece of creation. There is so much in an onion that you might miss if you don't give it reverence. Robert Farrar Capon spent twelve pages writing about an onion in *The Supper of The Lamb*. Can you choose one mundane activity and pursue it slowly? Sabbath is about treating the smallest objects in our life with the attention they deserve.

My best advice, then, to is to pay attention to what brings delight (*menuha*) and pursue it. What feels wasteful? Only you can answer that. And that's why Sabbath looks a little different for everyone. Most Sabbath days I start to get jittery around noon. Some days I crank up the lawn mower or weed eater. I hike. It feels good to be outside. Is my sweat a protest against resting? Or is it a means to deeply enter my body and my body the natural world? It must depend on my mindset—that is, whether the activity is done out of compulsion or freedom. If I work because I covet someone else's lawn, then I'm still enslaved. Sabbath is manifest when I am free to move for no other reason than God's delight.

Here's one idea: Put a puzzle together. Puzzles are a form of resistance to the capitalization of our activities. You don't even have to glue it together when you're done. Immediately take it apart and put it back in the box. Try taking a beautiful picture and not posting it to social media. That must be even more wasteful than puzzles.

In the evening, you might start by allowing yourself to watch a little television or you might allow yourself to turn off the television and sit on the porch with a book. But if the book becomes your taskmaster, you could switch to the television. Or vice versa. Perhaps you will choose to go for a walk instead of a run. Then again, maybe you will remain still as a form of resistance to the pharaoh that demands you to count your calories.

By the way, it's okay to amputate your phone from your body for an evening, a morning—then, an entire day. You can reattach it later with few repercussions. Influencers will keep posting photographs whether or not you're there to perceive them. The withdrawals can be painful, so it's best to keep close friends around for company. Your spouse, your kids, your parents will notice that you're looking them in the eyes when they're talking.

Then, when you really want to get good at keeping time, allow yourself to be interrupted. Look, I know that this is upper-level stuff, and I regularly fail the exam. But is there anything more subversive than interruptions? Being open to interruptions means you believe you can receive God in any moment—especially when God hasn't reserved a table in your calendar.

You might have to put down the planner for the day. "The opposite of grace is the planner," says my friend. Planner people are really estimable. Their past is crossed off with a check mark, the present is going according to plan, and the future is written down in ink. These are the people who really have their shit together, but you don't have to be one—especially on the Sabbath day. A color-coordinated life is usually bad at accepting interruptions. Henri Nouwen wrote that another priest told him, "I have always been complaining that my work was constantly interrupted; then I realized that the interruptions were my work."[11]

This seems to be the way God works—interrupting people with road trips, pregnancies, and dreams in the night. It's never convenient. Lives are flipped upside down. Uprooted. Or they take a hard U-turn. But even interruptions can become delightful in the kingdom of God. C. S. Lewis writes, "The great thing, if one can, is to stop regarding all the unpleasant things as interruptions of one's 'own', or 'real' life. The truth is of course that what one calls the interruptions are precisely one's real life—the life God is sending one day by day: what one calls one's 'real life' is a phantom of one's own imagination."[12]

Christianity asks us to be wasteful and profligate—to take a break from efficiency and embrace every moment and interruption as an opportunity to see God's face in a new and unexpected way. It hurts, and then it might save us from the ditch of self-importance, busyness, and anxiety. Something outside of us touches or calls to us, and we have the choice whether we want to stop and listen. It's risky, because it can throw your whole day or life off-balance. Yet the interruption might be a flash mob of joy on an ordinary Tuesday. Not always. But sometimes. They are at least a reminder that you are not the author of your own life.

Finally, you'll put your head down at night, possibly earlier than usual because you've run out of activities. This is good, too. Sleep is a mini death to yourself. Even sleep can be made holy when you fall asleep trusting that God will pick up where you left off. Put your head down, give yourself to God, and let the hours tick away as your life evaporates as a vapor given to God.

· · · · · · · · · · · · · · · · · ✦ · · · · · · · · · · · · · · · · ·

Someone this week might tell you, "There's not enough time in the day." And that's true. There is an unfinished quality to life—births unwitnessed, trips not taken, relationships left broken. There might not be enough time to travel to all fifty states or every continent. Life is too short to read everything you want to read. Unfortunately, I'll never eat the fifty best tacos in America. There's always more to see and experience. You will miss out.

God knows this as well as anyone else. God so desperately wanted our time to be made holy that God entered time in flesh and blood. The eternal was made finite. And God said, "Your time is my time." God lived with us until we ended his time. Then on the third day, he rose and made more. In the resurrection, God gave time back to us. Resurrected time means we have all the time in the world because we have been freed from time's chains.

If that's true, then there is always time to waste.

FOUR

GOD AND TABLES

Setting the Table
You Are What You Eat

I can describe few of my childhood dinners in detail. That's not to say they were unimportant. I can only describe a handful of worship services, too. All I know is that I'm a better person because of them. Ten thousand hours of passing salt, complaining, laughing, and making small talk will change you, whether you realize it or not.

My memories of the kitchen are idyllic—Norman Rockwell—mundane and beautiful, comprised of Tyson chicken strips and homemade marinara.[1] As a kid, I regularly sat at the kitchen counter while heat broke down the sugar molecules in the onions as they bathed in a pool of hot oil. The air was filled with a sweet aroma. Science makes life smell so good. In the morning, Mom and Dad lingered over the last drop of coffee from the pot (this was when newspapers were still delivered to mailboxes). In the evening, we held hands and said, "God is great. God is good," and everyone put dishes into the washer. Later at night, we gathered at the counter for late-night discussions and reminiscing.

None of this is entirely accurate. Memories are deceptive. Our kitchen was also a broken place; there was a crack down the center of the table. The table was a square instead of a circle, with sides and sharp edges. It was an area that exacerbated our culture's hierarchies and power structures—a place where dads cook with fire but not flour. Moms, meanwhile, are supposed to do everything else and also clean while settling for a chicken wing and the occasional compliment; "This tastes better than last time." Resentment and exhaustion were palpable in the kitchen as we all consumed the dead to live another day.

As a parent, I've realized the full extent of its difficulty. I now know why many families traded tables and conversations for trays and televisions. The television is a free babysitter. Meanwhile, the table demands attention and work. My wife and I stop every Saturday to think about next week's schedule: what we will eat and how we will come by the ingredients. Then, my wife or I must carve out the time to prepare what we dreamed up on a Saturday morning. Chicken Parmesan? On a Thursday? I'm not a bachelor trying to woo anyone.

When my kids turned one and three years old, the dinner table became a cold, dark place of weeping and gnashing of teeth. Getting the kids to eat was a hostage situation. The question "What's for dinner?" was more of a threat than a question. There was always a bathroom emergency, food was thrown on the floor, and the dishwasher was never loaded afterward. We argued about the menu until we threw in the towel, gave the kids the iPad, and heated up some chicken nuggets.

"Tomorrow, you are all cooking your own dinner," I said (and still say today).

It's an empty threat. Despite its challenges, the dinner table might be crucial for becoming a family. And so, we persevere, hoping the table can teach us something about grace and patience.

Wine helps.

They say, "You are what you eat." It's true. I'm unsure I'd know who I am without the dinner table. It's where our identities are transmitted through oral and written recipes. As a child, the dinner table was the theater where our family stories came to life—a catechesis into the Llewellyn-Snider lineage.

Anthropologist Claude Lévi-Strauss said the table is where we transform nature into culture—matter becomes a vehicle for story. Whenever we slapped Velveeta cheese between two pieces of bread, my dad would say, "Your grandfather worked in the Kraft factory." The story was retold with an underlying message: Work hard. Take nothing for granted. We learn the myth of a nation through the myth of the family—it's a story of Emersonian self-reliance, where anyone can pull themselves up by their bootstraps.

Food always means more than calories and nutrition. Isn't this why every food blogger tells a story before the recipe? One day, your grandma accidentally spills something in her braising liquid before Sunday worship. You come back to her house after worship and eat the most delicious shredded pork you've had in your life. Ever since, the family has eaten pork braised in Dr Pepper on Sunday afternoons. A deep, spiritual memory is incarnated in the material and tastes so good.

It's odd—we're scared to impose values and beliefs on our children, but then we go right ahead and foist our histories into their mouths. You can research lineage online or follow the transmission of dinner recipes until you end up at a Dutch table in Pennsylvania. No plate of food is created ex nihilo; instead, the family history is served in the bowl. Every bite joins us to our parents, which binds them to theirs. It might also join us to a church potluck one hundred years ago when recipes were passed down with a side of Jesus. My family is the kind of people who eat salad for dessert. "You will know us by our bowls of spring mix," we say with pride.

The Judeo-Christian tradition creates a people defined by tables and the food placed upon them. Isn't this why reading through the Israelites' food menu is so interesting? Jews who observe kashrut are forbidden to eat all kinds of interesting things: fish without fins and scales, and mammals that don't chew their cud. Dairy and meat can't be served together. The dietary laws forbid the Jewish people from eating animals that have been inhumanely slaughtered or those that have died from old age.

Pompous Christians scoff at the particularity, or the apparent arbitrariness, of their antiquated recipes. No shrimp or pork? Who cares about what we put into our mouths? A people who want to know who they are, that's who. They are a people who want to become holy—set apart and dedicated to God. And holiness requires attention—especially to matters of life and death.

There is a good rationale for many of the restrictions and admonitions. The Jewish codes of preparation insist on compassion. Could it be that Jews don't eat fish without scales or fins because they perceive them to be more vulnerable? And thus strive to be the kind of people who care for the weak?[2] Rabbi Arthur Waskow observed that separating meat from milk is a way of recalling the dissection between life (milk) and death (meat).[3] In other words, the Jews are a particular kind of people because they refuse to put cheese on beef burgers. They believe life is a gift.

Stanley Hauerwas, a theologian notorious for being provocative, quotes a Jewish friend as saying, "Any religion that does not tell you what to do with your pots and pans and genitals cannot be interesting."[4] The pots and pans give you an identity. And thus, the kitchen is a place for shared mission and work, a liturgy that bestows purpose and belonging. Your body isn't just yours; it's part of a larger body that gathers around the table.

I wonder whether we reflect deeply enough on the values of the table. What do we lose when we don't think about the ritual of eating? When we trade family recipes for frozen meals and premade dinners, are our stories cheapened and commoditized by money, convenience, and immediate gratification? How can we proclaim a gospel of communion in a culture of isolation?

The dinner table transforms us into a different kind of people—like a slow cooker that gently simmers us into something more tender and delicious. We develop patience bite after bite and argument after argument. We pray and say thank you. Recognizing the food on the table is a microcosm of attentiveness that evolves into reverence for all the material things that sustain us and give us life. We are a people of respect. I know the casserole tastes like a glob of mayonnaise. Eat it. You've surely heard the story about the cheese factory. Listen politely. Where do you learn how to share? You learn it best when there is only one piece left of Grandma's pecan pie, and it's your little brother's favorite.

Your home is your first sanctuary, a domestic church that mediates the presence of God and bestows identity. If that's the case, then the dinner table is your first altar where you learn to lay down your life for the ones you hold dear. And in return, you receive the grace that will sustain you in every moment of hunger.

Thanksgiving
Noticing the Blessings

One of the most important rituals of the table is thanksgiving. Most meals I've consumed, as far back as I can remember, have been marked with gratitude.

Thankfulness, for me, is not a natural disposition. I'm fairly certain I'm not alone in this. Naturally thankful people are annoying people. You know this, too. Today I saw someone smiling in the middle of a traffic gridlock. I wanted to throw a peppermint at their window. Think of the person in your life who always has a compass to the bright side. "I'm better than I deserve," they say. These are the golden retrievers and the Ted Lassos of the world. There is never scarcity. Always abundance. They live blissfully ignorant of the true state of the world. They wag their tails as the world heats beyond a sustainable temperature.

I ought to try to do better.

The Jewish tradition has prayers to mark every moment of their day with thanksgiving. Each day, when their eyes break through the crust and open for the first time, they pray, "I am thankful before You, living and enduring King, for You have mercifully restored my soul within me. Great is Your faithfulness."[1]

It's a beautiful prayer—the kind of thing I should say, even the kind of thing I aspire to say when I get up every morning. It's not what I actually say. My prayer is generally something like this: "Oh God! The kids are up." In case there is confusion, that is not an exclamation of anticipation for the start of another day. It's a lament that my soul has awoken my body from its death-like sleep.

Is the Mr. Coffee gurgling yet?

There's a list of things that must be done before the day can be started. The coffee beans must be ground to a fine dust, leaving a black residue reminiscent of soil on my hands. The mound will have to make its way into the hot water bath. On second thought, I'll shove a K-Cup into the machine and pop the lid down. I throw the plastic cup into the trash, which will go to a landfill. Slices of ham are rolled into cylinders and put in Tupperware along with crackers and fruit. A bag of muffins is mindlessly eaten to the tune of a morning cartoon. Kids are pinned down like alligators and wrestled into clothes. No, that shoe is on the wrong foot. Switch them. The youngest's diaper leaks. We forgot to change him. Do I need to carry you down the stairs, or will you walk?

No one sits at the table together. We're on our way.

Turns out that ingratitude is easy—just don't pay attention. I've already paraded by a whole slew of blessings while marching toward work. Every morning is made easier, if not possible, by countless hands from all over the globe. Martin Luther King Jr. put it this way: "Before you finish eating breakfast in the morning, you've depended on more than half the world. This is the way our universe is structured. It is its interrelated quality."[2] We're not self-made people, not one of us. Nothing merely appears with the swipe of a card or a push of a button. What we have comes from others and, more often than not, at their expense.

The coffee beans were selected, picked, and roasted by someone. The bag said Ethiopia. The baby's hand wrapped around my finger while I was giving him the bottle, which was less important than finishing that article for sermon preparation. The ham roll-ups were once a living animal, but who can make that connection after all the processing and packaging? It's hard to believe her sweater was once cotton, growing in a field somewhere before being sent to a factory.

We are "lucky" not to realize this—we live in a fast-food world where everything is cheap, anonymous, and expedient. The one thing you lose with affluence is humility; without humility, you lose dependence. The more you have, the less you think you need another person. The more you have, the more you believe you deserve. Why should we care about ecology when produce magically arrives at the grocery and water out of a faucet? The best we can do is give thanks for abstract generalities like "pig" or "farmer" or "textile manufacturer." Fossil fuels? Bad. Recycling? Good. Carbon footprint? Monitor. We are no longer mindful of our connection to the rich web of life that sustains our living.

The beginning of the day sets the standard for the rest. No one has time to read about what kind of chemicals are preserving the food, the thousands of miles a strawberry must travel before it reaches our mouths, the soul of the farmer who tended to the crop like a nurturing mother. The earth exists for our consumption, and we take from it mindlessly without giving back.

Ignorance is bliss.

A remedy to all this is thankfulness. Gratitude reminds us of who we are—creatures of the dirt, bound together with soil and flesh for better and worse.

German pietist and philosophical traditions have a phrase that captures this sentiment: "denken ist danken," which means "to think is to thank."[3] In other words, no thinking, then no thanking. The two are inseparable. Thanking is predicated on the hard work of thinking, paying attention, and noticing. You likely won't become thankful unless you set aside time to think—to confess your hurried, mindless way of life. But the reverse is also true. A posture of thankfulness determines a proper disposition toward the world. We think more clearly when we are thankful, as we notice the interrelated quality of our lives and the reality that we are not the story's main character.

Can we start with food? Food is always more than energy—proteins, carbohydrates, and sugars—that can sustain you for a few hours before your next dose of fuel. The food might have come from a grocery store, parking lot, or restaurant, but it likely originated somewhere else long before it reached your store or table. Look deeply into your plate and become cognizant enough to see the chicken that gave its life; remember the farmers that grew and picked the potatoes.

One of my favorite barbecue restaurants plasters the name of the slaughtered pig on a large wooden sign over the open kitchen. One day, we ate Rosalie, who hailed from a small farm in eastern North Carolina (I realize this is a Portlandia sketch). And yet, the sign honors the "pigness of the pig," to quote Joel Salatin, and is a reminder that something must die for us to eat. Sacrifice is inevitably a part of our eating. My life is made possible, in part, by Rosalie and those who cared for her. As Norman Wirzba says, "How do we become worthy of receiving another's death?"[4]

One of the best habits my parents instilled in me was the (perfunctory) mealtime blessing: God is great, God is good, let us thank God for our food. Out of all the beautiful table liturgies in the Christian tradition, this one made its way to most dinner tables around the country. But it's better than the Superman blessing (if this is unfamiliar, consider yourself blessed). Many days, it feels like a drawn-out way of saying "Ready, set, go." Yet it bestows familiarity with habit and unity through its resonance with other Christians. It's one small window to practice being human.

The family prayer has evolved since I've had children of my own. Today, my family of four sits at the table; we light a candle, pray, and ask each other, "What was your best today?" Posing the question makes us reflect on the day—it's a moment of Ignatian spirituality where we are forced to rewind through our days and fast forward. It's said that silent gratitude doesn't do anyone any good. Again, this is not natural for me, but it works because of peer pressure. If my children can remember playing "family" on the playground, then I can think of one person, place, thing, experience, or thought that brought me joy or showed me the face of God. There are two rules: Offer something specific, and lament is permitted as long as it's not habitual. We become thankful, even if only for the most mundane parts of the day:

I had a nice commute home today; the podcast was interesting.

I had a break between patients. I read my novel.

I might even offer proleptic gratitude for the meal: Our overcooked pork sure as hell will be better than the disaster that preceded it.

Gratitude is the practice of seeing what is all around us with a different set of eyes. Can you see life as a gift from God? Yes, I know you got stuck in traffic, received too many emails, and will later chauffeur your children through the city until the evening. Start with food and work toward human beings; don't be overzealous. Food is a microcosm of one's relationship to all matter. It's how we stop taking the world for granted and acknowledge our proper place in it—our sustenance from God and one another.

It's no wonder that the meal celebrated in the Christian tradition is called *Eucharist*, which means "to give thanks." In many church traditions, there is a long prayer that precedes receiving the bread and wine that is called "The Great Thanksgiving." In the prayer, God is given thanks for the blessings of creation, redemption, and sanctification.

"Lift up your hearts with joy," we say as to delight in the goodness of a world with garlic and onions, ripe strawberries and plump tomatoes, bread and wine. We confess our mindless living—the degradation of soil and lives: "We have not loved you with our whole heart . . . and we have not heard the cry of the needy." In turn, we are reoriented to the world as creatures who inhabit creation as a gift, totally reliant on one another for survival and health. The bread and the wine are a reconciliation back into a common life together, where everyone is interrelated and no one is estranged. The Eucharist begins with the transformation of the mind so we might receive the transformation of our bodies and lives.

Re-creation starts with thanksgiving.

No one has looked back on their lives and realized they wasted it with too much gratitude. The opposite is more likely. The more time you spend in thanksgiving, the deeper each moment becomes. Blessings are multiplied in their remembrance. It starts at the dinner table by spending the extra sixty seconds to pay attention—look around the table and relish in the web of life that is bound together. There has never been a moment like it, and there never will be another. If that is something we can muster up monthly at worship or nightly in our homes, then it might spread to all parts of our lives. And we'll no longer be able to think without thanking.

Anamnesis
Re-membering Christ

Recently, I took a piece of paper and jotted down a list of my favorite meals, a practice I recommend to anyone who needs a quick serotonin hit. The smells and tastes flooded my consciousness—the people and places were not far behind. The first meals that materialized from the recesses of my history were not necessarily the most delicious. Some of them were profoundly un-delicious.

I remembered my wife's first post-birth meal when I fed her bites of steak while my daughter received one of her first meals from my wife's chest. It was one of our first acts as a new family, peppered with the joy and exhaustion of dependency and self-sacrifice. Once, with sun-chaffed lips, I devoured a pizza into my tired body after a seventy-five-mile hike. The grease did my malnourished body no favors. Another time, friends and I ate Saint Peter's fish, a kind of tilapia, on the Sea of Galilee. Simon and Andrew caught these, or a similar species, before they became fishers of people, casting their poles two thousand years to catch us. Students scavenged for money and brought my wife and me tacos when we lost our jobs; I won't quickly forget their generosity. I took my college romantic interest to Burger King when her boyfriend broke up with her. Later, she became my wife, and I haven't taken her to Burger King since.

ANCIENT EXTRAVAGANCE

I have few clear memories of meals eaten alone. The burgers I consumed while speeding down the highway never left a lasting impression. Nor did the Lean Cuisines I used to eat in front of the television. The one exception might be Cook Out milkshakes. I've found that when I drive to get ice cream late at night, I enjoy it regardless of my company. But my point still stands: We have to eat to survive, of course, and surviving is most delicious when it's done in community (ice cream excluded).

Most of the time, the people around the table are just as important as what is on the plate. Can you tell the story of your best friend without referencing food? Food is the adhesive that connects us one to another.

Food happens to be one of the best love languages we have as humans. Feeding and being fed by others is a declaration of love. Don't we create someone's favorite dish to say "I love you" (or to say "I made a big mistake")? We deliver casseroles when we have no words for friends deep in grief. The best way we know to thank our loved ones at a wedding ceremony is with dinner and dancing and booze.

Likewise, our human limitation is satiated with grace when we receive food from others. We unfurl our fingers, cup our hands, and receive our fill in mind, body, and spirit. A doughnut waiting on your desk means someone noticed you had a rough week. A friend's attentiveness sweetens the bite, unlike any sugar. Open hands are a gesture that communicates the truth about our lives: We need to be fed.

God also communicates love through and around food. This explains why Jesus was a prolific eater. Someone once pointed out that Jesus eats his way through the Gospels. There are over fifty references to food in the Gospel of Luke. What would it be like, by the way, to imagine Jesus not thin and muscular but chubby—his stomach hanging over the cincture that's tied around his waist? Here is a God who is full rather than famished.

Did Jesus eat more often than we do? Or did his first followers best remember their times with Jesus that involved food? The Gospels can't be told without referencing food. Jesus's first miracle in the Gospel of John was taking water barrels and creating wine. When he rose from the dead, hungry from defeating sin and death, he started a fire and cooked some fish. In between birth and death, Jesus made secular tables holy, blurring the boundaries between the sacred and the profane.

Hungry people followed him, hoping to get a taste of the bread he offered. On a hillside, thousands of them did. He called himself "bread"—essential to life.

Jesus's best sermon illustrations were about dinner parties, because that's where he spent his time. The marriage of heaven and earth, the perfect union and communion of God and all God's children, is celebrated with a great feast. And so he taught the disciples about the proper table manners in the kingdom of God, including where you sat, who you invited, and what you're supposed to do when no one shows up. Then, he enacted that metaphor and used the table to usher in the kingdom of God. The Pharisees criticized his behavior, calling him a glutton, drunkard, and friend of sinners.

"Do this in remembrance of me," he said at the last meal he shared with his best friends. Isn't it fitting that Jesus wanted to mark the end of his time on earth with a meal? His willingness to eat everywhere, with anyone, got him killed.

It can be hard to pin down Jesus as the Spirit carries him over the face of the earth. But he promises he'll always be found when two or three gather around a table in his name.

· · · · · · · · · · · · · · · · ✦ · · · · · · · · · · · · · · · ·

The meal we call Holy Communion (or, depending on your theological tradition, the Lord's Supper or Eucharist) is the vehicle for God's communion with humanity in the person of Jesus, who eats with us and offers himself as food. Communion is one of the ways we have ritualized Christ's presence at dinner tables.

As a child, I wasn't sure what to make of it. We received communion once a month, a compromise between those who wanted it weekly and those who wanted it quarterly. Here's what I knew about communion: Once a month, I had to walk in front of the church to dip bread in juice and pray to God that I didn't choke or start coughing (I was an anxious child). I also knew that we could expect to wait for a table at El Potro after church was over.

It's one of the stranger parts of the Christian faith. We claim to eat the body and drink the blood of our dead savior—look, that's not out of bounds for a future Discovery Channel documentary on cannibalism. The earliest opposition to Christianity included this very indictment—these people eat dead people. Not to mention that we all eat from the same loaf and drink from the same cup—a renewed complication for people who have suffered from a global pandemic.

Throughout seminary I worked at a youth development center, a juvenile detention and rehabilitation facility for young men who had gotten in trouble with the law. It was the kind of place a seminary student felt uncomfortable in, and the type of place in which Jesus said he would dwell. One week, a friend was assisting in the celebration of Holy Communion for the young men. Right in the middle of the liturgy, one of the boys shouted, "I'm not eatin' that bread. That motherf*cker put his hands all over it."

Christ is present—even there. Especially there.

Our God is Immanuel, God with us, which is why the church calls the meal a sacrament—an efficacious sign that bestows the very thing it points to, God's presence. "You are what you eat," goes the adage—we eat Jesus, or with Jesus, to become like Jesus. Theologians have long argued about how exactly Jesus is present in wine and bread. Saint Francis said, "For our salvation, Jesus hides in a piece of bread." Maybe that's all that needs to be said.

> Just as this broken loaf was scattered over the hill as grain,
>   and, having been gathered together, became one;
> in like fashion, may your church be gathered together
>   from the ends of the earth into your kingdom.[1]

In church parlance, we call this anamnesis, or the remembrance of Christ. Some take Jesus's words at their most literal and believe the bread and wine become Christ himself, even while looking and tasting the same (you'll need a quick lesson in Aristotelian metaphysics to understand this). Others say the bread and the wine retain their natural properties, but Christ is present nonetheless. Still others hold that Communion is only a meal of remembrance—a symbol of what Christ has already done and accomplished.

Every theology of Communion is intentional, and we ought to be slow to condemn others' practices of it. Still, we can, eventually, disagree. I'm partial toward a theology that argues that Christ is actually present.

Flannery O'Connor once said, "If it's just a symbol, to hell with it."[2] If I'm going to spend an hour of my life sitting on a hard pew, then I'm going to need more than a symbol of Christ's love and sacrifice. Jesus not only died, but he was also raised to new life. A ritual of memorial captures the former but not the latter. Christ is alive, raised to heaven, and spread throughout the entire earth. There's no need to capitulate to a theology of symbolism when Christ is risen. You'll find him—very much alive—in the place that brought him joy: tables.

I lament that these mental theological differences keep our denominational bodies apart. We sacrifice the presence of Christ for institutional rules and theological uniformity. This is the prioritization of principles over encounter and a loyalty to ideas rather than Christ. Our rules about where God is and isn't can distract us from the God who is always revealed in our neighbors—particularly the ones we don't like or agree with. To segregate an altar and a table is to divide Christ right down the middle.

My current place of worship offers an alternative. We gather weekly as a congregation of denominational refugees—Catholics, Methodists, Episcopalians, and even Baptists. But together, we have found sanctuary in a place where people no longer follow Apollos or Paul (Luther or Wesley or Augustine). We follow Christ, instead, having been freed from the fortress theologies that separate us from one another. Each week, we come to the table, disagreeing about what we're doing at the table in the first place, but receive Christ all the same. Our minds don't have to be of one accord for our bodies to join in communion. In eating and drinking, we dissolve and sink into union with the greater body of Christ.

The Scriptures have little to say about how Jesus is present in Eucharist. The early church seemed to think Jesus meant he was present in the ordinary partaking of food and drink for the body. These first followers of Christ celebrated Communion as a full meal, not just a pinch and a shot. Today, many churches walk to the altar to the tune of a death march, thinking of Christ's sacrifice. Yet the early church gathered on resurrection day to celebrate the best way they knew how—food, song, and storytelling. Sharing their food and lives, they redefined their communal life through all the tables Christ graced.

I sometimes wonder if we've missed the point of Communion when it's overly ritualized. I adore the Communion ritual; the words take me on a voyage past altars and tables that brings me closer to the first table where Jesus sat with his disciples. I've even committed the liturgy to heart as poetry for my soul. But I rarely leave a service of Word and Table thinking that I've seen my neighbor and come away with a deeper appreciation for the earth's goodness. Does the ritual really make us mindful of our eating and our dependence on one another and God? Or is the altar merely a self-check-out counter? Are the elements of bread and wine a personal serving of God?

What if it's the ordinary meal infused with Eucharistic character that's holy? The meal Jesus blessed the night before his execution was a full meal. And it was also a commonplace one. Bread and wine—not lobster and pheasant.[3] These commonplace ingredients became the vessels to receive the God who is all around us. And so, the early church celebrated Christ in the ordinary. They drank bad wine, ate bread on paper plates, and told embarrassing stories with their elbows on the table (I'm guessing). Arguments, debates, and clean-up were imbued with the presence of Christ.

If this is the case, then the church potluck is one of the most historic practices of church communion. I've rarely been to a potluck where I wasn't encouraged to make small talk, inquire about recipes (how much butter is in this thing?), and serve my story to others for the goodness of the body. I meet Christ in the present, not the past, through neighbor and the earth's goodness. The holy meal is our full embodiment of the *imago Dei*, the image of God.

· · · · · · · · · · · · · · · · ✦ · · · · · · · · · · · · · · · ·

There was a season in my life when I gathered every other week to share a potluck at a brewery as a form of worship and communion. Millennials! We offered prayers of thanksgiving for malts, yeast, hops, and water. And then, we passed the buffalo chicken. Soon, we moved our gatherings to one another's houses. We added people here and there. Like any biological family, we didn't choose one another. A potluck of people—friends,

friends of friends, and friends of friends of friends. Infants and babies. Twentysomethings, thirtysomethings, and fortysomethings with different tastes in theology, politics, and food. But we could all use more recipes to get us through life.

Being the church is a little like learning to eat broccoli and drink black coffee, which means you can develop a taste for people even if you didn't choose them. I assure you that it's possible. Even a Midwesterner can learn to love sweet tea and grits (it takes a lot of practice). Sometimes, we must start by smothering them with cheese and adding too much creamer. But the goal, the proper end, is to learn to enjoy them for who they are and not who we want them to be, even if it means reading the ingredients on the back of boxes and checking for food allergies.

The good news is that the reverse is also true—maybe you feel like you're the broccoli, and you're afraid that no one could ever possibly love you. But then, everyone shows up at the table again, night after night. The dinner table is the best place to taste another's life and then taste again until you can understand the complexities a bit better.

One family always cooked pink beans and rice. It was a Brazilian-inspired dish with cumin and turmeric, perfected after years of shared tables. We covered it with a cilantro sauce. It was a dish formed from a childhood spent in Brazil—something I couldn't cook for myself even if I wanted to (which I didn't). But at the table, we consume and are consumed by another culture, history, and family. The table is where strangers become friends—taking an extension of another person into our very bodies to be digested and transformed into new life. Today, our family eats pink beans and rice once a week. Have we become honorary Brazilians?

There's a sense in which this meal is at least as Eucharistic as the meal on Sunday mornings, as Christ joins us in the ordinary rituals of praying, storytelling, and eating. Paying attention to the ingredients of food and life, we are absorbed into one another's lives.

I understand that this all sounds sentimental. Eat together. Christ will be present. It'll be easy, I tell you. Don't be fooled. Many nights, I wanted to be at the table, but I knew it was a chore. My kids were prone to meltdowns of cosmic proportions halfway through dinner. Food was thrown, obviously. But someone would graciously pick up a kid, plop him in her lap, and continue asking nosy questions about God, faith, and global warming. Bless her—she was holy.

Still today, I end up around a table with friends most weeks, and it's not an accident. It's scheduled and written in a little box on a calendar. We make the effort because we know it's where Christ is present, drawing us closer to one another and deeper into the soil of our constitution. Communion is the converse of a typical meal—we don't digest it. Instead, it digests us and makes us into the body of Christ.[4] By remembering Christ, we literally re-member him as fingers on hands and hands on arms.

The magic of Communion isn't just that the bread becomes Christ but that we become bread for one another and thus become Christ. The meal is anamnesis, our re-membrance.

Epiclesis
A Prayer

"Dominus meus et Deus meus,"
cried Thomas when he
recognized The One before him—scarred and risen.
The crucified one ascends and carries the scars
born on earth into the core of God's self.
Heaven is on earth, and
earth in heaven. Or,
if God is there, then
God is also here.
Martin Luther said God is just as present in cabbage soup as bread blessed by a priest. Soup and bread. No hocus pocus or secret combination of words is necessary. Not even a pulpit or man or building. We don't have to look at the sky to find God but look horizontally at the burning bushes—the people we meet and places we find ourselves situated in. God is just as present in the newborn baby as in the intensive care unit or in all our acts of love that sustain each other's lives.
There is no miraculous change in the earth.
Just a miraculous change in us
when we realize
the gift of God is all around.
Stoke the fire in your heart.
And adjust your sails.
When we learn that God is present there,
in bread and wine,
we might come to realize that
God is also present
here.

Take, Bless, Break, Give
Extending the Table

Most churches I know think they serve the best meals. Even the churches that serve family recipes from the back of Betty Crocker boxes. They are deluded. "Baptists are known for eating," they say. Yes, but so are Methodists, Lutherans, and Presbyterians. New Christians who decry formal worship still seek Christ at brunch tables over chicken, waffles, and mimosas. Catholic worship, known as Mass, culminates with Christ being smelled, tasted, felt, and heard with bread and wine. Their meal becomes Christ—that's arguably the best meal you'll ever ingest (even if there is no cream of mushroom soup).

What's clear is that eating together is not a denominational distinctive; it's a mark of the church universal. If you are a human being, then you eat. And Christians care about what's on the plate (often excluding nutrition and sustainability). Less often, we think about the people around the table. Even fewer denominations and congregations brag about the kinds of people they eat with. Our food insulates us from the world more than it integrates us into the world.

Eating with friends and family is hardly an accomplishment. We gravitate to those who have the same color of skin and the same amount in the bank. It's written deep into our history because it's written deep into our

ANCIENT EXTRAVAGANCE

biology—find safety in tribes of likeness and fear the other. And so we lounge in the presence of those who share our life experiences and affirm our worldviews.

The difference is that Jesus ate with everyone, especially those without a seat at the table. Uniformity and homogeneity are not hallmarks of the kingdom of God. Christians are distinctive, instead, due to the kind of people we invite to the table. What if the best indicator of our spiritual health is not based on our Sunday attendance but on whether we eat with people who don't look like us, live like us, or pray like us?

✦

Every summer during high school, my youth group boarded two fifteen-passenger vans and traveled eight and a half hours from outside Savannah, Georgia, to the Hinton Rural Life Center in Hayesville, North Carolina—from grains of beach sand to layers of clay and silt and gentle sandstone slopes. The eight hours of driving and listening to nineties boy bands were tolerable by the prospect of meeting girls. This is how service trips often work: You sign up because of a romantic interest but end up meeting Jesus instead. It's the best bait and switch ever devised.

One year, my group was assigned to work with an elderly woman on her dilapidated house. She lived alone in a home that reeked of animal odors from untrained pets. It was musty. I remember this clearly because it was the first time I held my nose in another person's living space. It's one thing to read about poverty or see it on television, but it's quite another thing to touch and smell it. I wondered if wearing a mask in another person's living space was polite. Is shielding your nose less offensive than shielding your eyes?

Our task was to put up drywall (because it's not at all offensive to ask untrained high schoolers to remodel homes). I stayed in my lane by measuring the Sheetrock for the few trained carpenters who knew what they were doing. As best as I can remember, we put up new walls. We might have even laid tile (crooked, of course). The work didn't leave an impression.

Here's what did: the large cucumber garden. Every day at noon, we took a break from snapping blue lines on sheetrock to sit down at the table together. She walked to her garden, picked cucumbers, and piled them up on a makeshift table—a big piece of plywood between two sawhorses.

"Y'uns want some salt on your cucumbers," she said in her Appalachian twang, whistling through the gaps between her teeth.

I didn't.

Who puts salt on their cucumbers? I later learned that this is the same kind of person who puts it on their watermelon. To be completely honest, I wanted the sandwich waiting for me inside my lunch sack. Or, as an alternative, I would have been happy to forgo the meal altogether. Best to get back to the Lord's work: putting up crooked drywall.

But she insisted. And the cucumbers kept coming.

Our group of six found seats on porch steps and rocks unearthed from the hard mountain clay. There, we were forced to slow down and do the kind of thing that makes for a good Christian—spend time with a stranger.

Our temptation as humans is to close off the table or restrict the number of chairs, but Jesus enters the party with a table leaf and some stools. I don't remember Jesus fixing many houses in Scripture, but I have read plenty of stories about him sharing life and food with lepers, lunatics, and demoniacs—the kinds of people that smell weird, are hard to talk with, and forget to show gratitude. It's best to remember that Jesus was constantly criticized for eating with the wrong people. His opponents were right. He did eat with sinners. And he still does. I know this because he eats with me.

The church has long debated who gets a seat at the Lord's Supper. In the book of Acts, the early church constantly encountered people with nowhere to belong, waiting on the outsider list. And the early church asks itself whether they can make more room. "Even them?" they ask. "The Gentiles, the non-Jews, the ones outside the covenant?"

Ew.

In one of my favorite stories, God instructed Cornelius, a Gentile believer, to send friends to Peter, a Jewish disciple, to ask for a meeting (see Acts 10). Cornelius was Italian, accustomed to a different diet of food, people, and God. If you're the kind of person who eats breadsticks and meatballs, then you're not automatically given a ticket into the new messianic Jewish fellowship.

God interrupted Peter's consciousness with a dream while these men were on their way to meet Peter. Peter had gone up to a roof to pray but began to get hungry. It's a literal and deep metaphorical hunger. He's hungry for food, but we later learn he is also hungry for God's will. And he received a dream: A sheet descended from heaven. And the sheet was filled with foods that a Jewish disciple would never eat—like pigs. Pigs are delicious to most of us, but they are inedible to Jews.

God told Peter the unthinkable, "Peter, rise, kill, and eat."

"But I can't eat bacon!" says Peter.

"Peter, it's time to eat bacon."

It takes Peter three times, his magic number, to get the point.

Cultural diversity, especially through food, is beautiful. The Jewish food menu helped the people of God retain their identity, values, and priorities. They knew their mission. We need people who make us feel safe in a world that can feel so dangerous. But when your food is used to exclude and alienate, you starve yourself. The dream isn't really about eating bacon. The dream is about the people who eat bacon. It's God's cafeteria curriculum 101: Break up the segregation. We are made one through Christ, not our obedience to food laws.

Do you want to desire the people whom God desires? Start with their food.

This, of course, upset some of the Jews. "So when Peter went up to Jerusalem, the circumcised believers criticized him, saying, 'Why did you go to uncircumcised men and eat with them?'" (Acts 11:2–3). In effect, Peter says, "I did not want to do this, but the Spirit made me do this." Willie Jennings says Peter was always a "reluctant visionary."[1] Besides sex, what is more intimate than eating with another person? Your jaws clench around flesh while your stomach gurgles as the acid breaks down and digests your sustenance. You struggle to think of something to discuss between each bite, a poppy seed wedged between your incisors.

Yet the Spirit drove the church—against all cultural, political, and religious purity—to eat with the people we don't want to eat with and thus invite them into the fullness of Communion.

One sign of salvation in the church was the dinner table. People who did not belong together shared a meal, becoming brothers and sisters in

Christ. It made no sense, unless Christ worked through the Spirit, creating hunger for people who didn't seem very appetizing. The table was a sphere of resistance to uniformity; it was a breathing space where hierarchy and division were subverted and a disruption to the geography of our belonging.

Our communion must unite the people most divided in the world into the sacred act of divine eating, where souls entwine as bread in wine.

The real reason why I didn't want salted cucumber is because I didn't want the person. It sounds harsh, I know. My rejection wasn't rooted in animosity but fear. I didn't know the protocol or table expectations. Exclusion can arise out of prejudice and discrimination but also out of insecurity. Life is easier when our social roles and expectations are clear: I was there to serve, not be served. I am the feeder. She is the fed. Too often, we use service to create a chasm between those serving and those being served.

But this woman would not let our service cancel out the potential friendship of being with one another in communion. In her invitation, she held up a mirror to my fundamental reality—that I was dependent. She wore her brokenness on the outside, while mine was carefully covered in expensive clothes, fake smiles, and a servant's heart. But my arrogance reeked worse than the house where she made her home. There is deep poverty when we try to fix another without being with another.

She was hungry. And I, too, needed to be fed. We are all simultaneously providing and being fed—all the time. Each of us is shaded by gift and need, bound up in the communion of power and depravity.

Sitting on our rocks and stoops, we sprinkled salt on our cucumbers. She gave us unsolicited gardening advice and talked about the year's crop. It was a good year for cucumbers. And the next day, we did it again. Then again. Until we left to go back home. I welcomed another, or one who is other, into my life because she had welcomed me into hers.[2] The salt cut the bitterness and brought out a new, fresh flavor.

Jesus instituted a new way of eating when he lifted a cup and broke bread. Christ gathers our shared humanity with four distinct actions—the fourfold pattern for every supper. He takes bread, blesses bread, breaks bread, and gives bread. Christ did this when he fed the five thousand, ate with his friends for his final meal, and sat with Cleopas after the resurrection. One theologian, Sam Wells, says this is what Jesus did with his whole life. God took human form, blessed us with ministry, was broken on the cross, and gave us life in the resurrection.[3]

The early Christian community defined their worship with this fourfold Eucharistic pattern. They knew that Jesus Christ was taking them and gathering them in the power of the Spirit. These people sat down at the table as individuals with their resources, hopes, dreams, prayers, and sin. But in the breaking of bread, Christ broke down all their barriers and blessed them with a new unity. And when they left the table, they had been given new life.

The table would be simpler if God had the same invitation list as you. God doesn't. And the greatest sin is to presume that we are the hosts of the dinner, the ones who create seating charts for the world. This is God's party, God's dinner table. God is always the host. We are merely servants and guests, lucky to find ourselves at the table. If we are to eat at Jesus's table, then we don't decide on the menu or customize the details to our preferences. The Jews and Gentiles shared a table and broke pita and drank wine. The different notes blended to make a harmony that neither could make alone. If we believe this, then there's a reason to have church. If not, then we should continue to sit with insiders and scapegoat those on the outside.

My work in the mountains was less about fixing houses and more about having my life broken wide open to receive grace through learning to enter the mystery of another's life. It's easier to do than to be, but doing doesn't save in the same way as being. Mission and incarnation are inseparable, as part of our mission always entails the beautiful, risky entangling of lives that are simultaneously poor and rich.

Every table is an opportunity to extend "The Great Thanksgiving" into our world. And the church is called to be the foretaste of the heavenly banquet where the church from every generation, tribe, people, and language gathers around the table as friends and companions.

In the meantime, what are we telling the world that God tastes like? Bitter? Salty or sour? Sweet? That elusive umami?

Maybe the taste is cucumber—at least in Appalachia.

FIVE

GOD'S EXTRAVAGANT GRACE

A Baptism
Called Beloved

When I stopped pretending that I liked goat cheese, my life took a turn for the better. For the longest time, I knew I was the kind of person who liked goat cheese, especially with strawberries and balsamic vinaigrette. It fit the persona that I had manicured. You know, I consume elitist things like goat cheese and Jonathan Franzen novels. But I never really liked either of them, and I eventually accepted that I didn't care to learn to like them.

One day, for no apparent reason, I just started telling people that I thought goat cheese tasted like cow cheese that had been eaten and regurgitated. We become more and less free as we age. Aging is a safe space in that way, a place where you don't have to pretend to like *Hamilton*, to quote one of my favorite television characters. There's no point in carrying around something that can be easily discarded when your back already aches from fractured relationships, dental issues, and climbing interest rates.

Life is lighter without the cheese.

Around the same time, I also began to stop reading books I didn't enjoy before I reached the halfway point. This was a big step for someone with an obsessive-compulsive desire to finish everything they started. Then I stopped checking the scores of sports teams I did not care about. Today, I haven't been to the gym for an entire year, my most extended hiatus since

I was seventeen. I am rapidly losing interest in the clothes I wear. This is exhilarating. Next stop, Hawaiian T-shirts and cargo shorts. I'm not sure what will happen after that. Crocs? When you no longer feel the need to impress others, do you become free enough to delete your social media? The sky is the limit.

It's exhausting to maintain a slew of interests, all meant to manufacture an identity that isn't really you. I've juggled identities, trying to keep them all up in the air without making a fool of myself for as long as I can remember. Who are you? Jock, nerd, creative, or religious? I'll take twenty-five percent of each, please. I must know the latest sports stats to be sporty enough for the jock crowd. Read *The New Yorker* and eat goat cheese and drink wine for the White liberal academics. Stay current on the latest music, novels, and graphic design for the nerds. And I'm in church weekly, reading theology daily. Even if I keep all these things in the air, it doesn't change the fact that I'm a clown who is juggling.

So much of our lives are staged to appease and impress real and imaginary people who care too much and, more often, not at all about our lives. It's hard to tell who is who, so we work to become the most perfect versions of ourselves at all times and places. The advantage, I suppose, is belonging—a tribe that serves as our fortress and safety net. In the process, we ignore who really matters, ourselves and God, though the voice of God is hard to separate from the voices of the people we want to please.

The most challenging part of Christianity is accepting that I have already been told who I am; I can do nothing to change the core of my identity. It doesn't even matter what face mask, armor, or costume I'm wearing. The playacting can stop because the very Someone who oversees all things seen and unseen thinks I am worthy of love. And guess what? There's even better news: It's true whether or not I have gained ten pounds, lost my ability to run a mile in under ten minutes, or have money in the bank account.

All I really needed to know about my life was there, in a little bowl of water, before I could utter a word or walk on my own two feet.

I was one month old when I was brought to Trinity Lutheran Church for my baptism. I wore a little blue bubble suit handed down from my older brother. Two pastors presided over the service, likely because I was such a terrible baby. There was my Pappy, who was a Methodist pastor, and the pastor of the Lutheran church, whom my mom described as a wimpy guy with a weak voice. From what I understand, the ritual of my baptism was indistinguishable from the last. They splashed some water on me. I cried. They pronounced the name of the Trinity: Father, Son, Holy Spirit. Big deal. Nothing out of the ordinary. Still, there was no moment quite like this one. I was held by particular sets of hands and touched by unique fingerprints; my cry was like no other. Every ordinary event can become exceptional through our mutual love.

Water is entirely ordinary, but it sustains all life. The sacraments, like baptism, remind us that God takes ordinary things—and ordinary moments—to save us and make us holy. Every baptismal font holds the same compound of hydrogen and oxygen atoms that nourish us in the womb and run through our veins. Water is the only satisfaction for a dry mouth and the foundation for complex and delicious food. It cleanses our children following an afternoon of marching through the forests; later, it becomes the bubble bath for the overworked mother or the sponge bath for the resident in the nursing home. God takes the most commonplace compound in our world, water, to give us the best news about our past, present, and future—cleansing, sustaining, and saving.

Baptism is the strange way Christ and the church have decided to make Christians. The word "baptism" only means "dipping," which means it's kind of like a spiritual bath. All our grime can be washed off with a little grace—even the most stubborn, hidden bits of dirt, like the kind that accrues in the crevices of your belly button. It's the first of many times throughout your life that God will pick up a washcloth and offer cleansing.

The Anabaptist tradition tells us we ought to wait until infants have grown into (semi) rational adults. "You ought to let them choose for themselves," some say. They make a good point. For a long time, infant baptism functioned as an imperial birth registry, creating and reinforcing one's in-group and national identity. Anabaptists remind us that Christians aren't created by birth but by decision—Christians make a defining commitment. No infant can count the cost and choose to follow Jesus.

While I acknowledge the hazards of dunking babies, I still put my two children under the water. Regardless of age, aren't we always infants in the faith? I'm not sure I've met a rational adult who would choose to die to self to follow a homeless rabbi.

It matters what syllables you decide to stress. Do we choose to mark our choice for God or God's choice for us? Before my daughter was baptized, I had family members ask: "When's the dedication?"

And every time, I had to respond, "It's a baptism. We don't dedicate. We baptize."

"Well, what's the difference?" they asked.

A dedication is something we do, but a baptism is something God does. And that's the difference. All we have to do is receive and acknowledge that grace. We get to choose many things in life, but we don't often get to choose what families we are born into or whether someone chooses to love us.

On the day of my baptism, I was given a felt banner made by my Meemaw that said, "Ryan is Jesus's child." There's nothing aesthetically pleasing about this banner. It's embarrassing in the wrong company. That's why I love it. I was named by God. I became a part of Christ's body before I could say the word *God*. God's grace goes before any action I would ever take; it's a gift of love that I will never earn nor merit. But with the help of those in my boat, I'd eventually learn to take my first step out of the water and say the words for myself, "I will follow."

In the Gospels, Jesus moves from the water of the womb to the waters of baptism almost seamlessly. His adult ministry begins at the water, as he's joined by an ensemble of people whose lives were inundated with chaos. Mark writes, "John the baptizer appeared in the wilderness, proclaiming a baptism of repentance for the forgiveness of sins. And the whole Judean region and all the people of Jerusalem were going out to him and were baptized by him in the River Jordan" (Mark 1:4–5). On that day, the Jordan River must have been teeming with xenophobes and addicts, adulterers and the sexually promiscuous, tax collectors and extortionists. Perhaps others appeared healthy and happy but harbored guilt or darkness deep in their souls.

Almost immediately, John criticizes his cousin's decision to get baptized. Why would Jesus need it? The church fathers and mothers remind us that Jesus wasn't baptized due to his sin but to sanctify the waters for the rest of us.[1] The earliest followers of Jesus were delivered together in the waters of the Jordan and adopted into the one family of God.

Jesus's baptism reveals that no Tower of Babel will reach to the heavens. Instead, God descends into the water—a womb and river. God is like a parent who reaches down into the bathtub to scrub a screaming toddler and then climbs in to be with her, soothe her, and show her all will be well. God came down—down—down until God was immersed into all the scum and algae of our world. In return, the world became immersed in all of God. In some early icons of Jesus's baptism, fish are pictured jumping out of the water in celebration as Jesus goes under. Join with all nature in manifold witness.

Israel's history is fulfilled at Jesus's baptism. The Spirit that hovered over the chaotic waters when the world was birthed is now hovering over Jesus's waterlogged body, bestowing a new creation. The dove Noah sent out when the ark floated on sea waves has returned with another olive branch—Jesus. Now he's at the Jordan River, that is, the same river the Israelites crossed to enter the promised land after being led by Moses through the Red Sea to freedom out of Egypt. Isaiah's prayer, "O that you would tear open the heavens and come down" (Isa. 64:1), is finally answered. Here's the point: Jesus creates order out of chaos, sets the captives free, and foreshadows peace.

Finally, God speaks from the heavens: "You are my Son, the Beloved; with you I am well pleased" (Mark 1:11). The subversive part of this story is that Jesus hasn't done anything yet. He hasn't given a sermon. The sick haven't been healed. Sins haven't been forgiven. The dead aren't being raised. It's like getting a trophy for participation.

Mark and the other Gospel writers tell us the identity of this man before he begins his work: Jesus is the Beloved One who stands amid our sin.

And he refuses to look away.

· · · · · · · · · · · ✦ · · · · · · · · · · ·

The world is more than ready to pronounce your identity, so it's best to get who you are clear as early as possible. At every baptism, the church will gather around a font or a feeding trough or a swimming pool or a river and pronounce the most important name you'll ever receive: Beloved. All the names that will threaten to steal your identity are proleptically put in the water and drowned. Notice what this means. Your worth is not based on your achievements, knowledge, or even your goodness or beliefs. It's not the house or the car. Forget about the likes on social media. These crucial names clothe you: Christian, a little Christ. Beloved, loved by God.

You are "Christ-ened," called by the name of Christ.

There is a paradox at the core of baptism: Everything changes, and nothing completely changes. There were no observable differences in my life. It did not make me a well-behaved baby. Nor did I suddenly sleep better. If baptism is efficacious, then it works slowly like a seed that is planted and still needs watering, a marriage that must be attended to, a child who grows into the life that waits for them. You must choose to renew the vows daily, if not hourly—sometimes by the minute. You say yes to God one day, then the next day, and then every day for the rest of your life.

The early Christians called themselves the people of the Way because the Christian life is not about arriving but always about becoming. Baptism, then, is not so much about the moment you arrive at the font, whether you are an infant or adult, but the subsequent time you spend climbing out of it. It's been said that baptism takes a minute to perform and a lifetime to fulfill. Baptism, like faith itself, is not just something we possess. It's something we grow into. That's true whether you were baptized at six months or sixty years.

I don't even remember the first time I confirmed what took place at my baptism. There was a time when I stood up in front of the church and told everyone "I'm in," but I started following Jesus long before that. To answer when I began following Jesus would be like asking when I started loving my parents. It happened, indeed, but not at any one moment. My conversion was less like the chrysalis of a caterpillar and more like the metamorphosis of a tadpole. It happened slowly, and the end product wasn't a beautiful butterfly so much as a frog with warts. If anyone is in Christ, there is new creation (but you're still a little slimy).

The central question is this: Can you live as one who has been baptized? Or will you spend the rest of your life pretending it never happened?

You have the freedom to accept God's love or reject it. But it doesn't change the fact that the whole Christian gospel could be summed up with God's first phrase to Jesus: "You are my dear child; I'm delighted with you."

There's nothing you have to do—and nothing you can do—to earn it. Once you receive this, you'll be free, too.

And we can both stop eating cheeses we don't like.

Confession of Doubt
Holding on When There's Nothing to Believe

One day, I was driving alone when I realized I might not believe in God anymore. I'm still not sure why. It wasn't intellectual; I was long past worrying about textual tensions, monks altering manuscripts, and Gospel accounts that don't always see eye to eye. I was never threatened by those who claimed that God was a projection of our humanity or that religion was wish fulfillment in cosmic proportions. A God made at least as much sense as no God. And the God of Israel and Jesus Christ told a better story than reductive materialism.

There's an adage that says you go bankrupt gradually and then all at once. I think that's the same way we lose our faith. It dies a little each day, maybe over a few years, until nothing is left. The image of a loaf of Communion bread comes to mind. The priest gives away pieces of the bread, pieces of God, until there are just crumbs scattered on a plate. One hand picks at it, then another, and another. One day, you'll arrive at the table, and the loaf is gone. You beg for a crumb of faith, like the woman who told Jesus that even dogs would eat the crumbs from the master's table, but God has no bread left to give out.

God's silence is the most excruciating form of pain imaginable. My faith was plunged into the darkness of Good Friday, the day Jesus was crucified. Good Friday is the one day of the year when the sun doesn't shine, even when the sun is out. The horror of the crucifixion story is spiritual torment as much as physical agony. Jesus was abandoned. "My God, my God, why have you forsaken me?" he cried out (Matt. 27:46).

Early Christians said Jesus became an atheist at this moment. He wasn't an intellectual atheist, of course. He was a spiritual atheist. He didn't have lukewarm faith. He had no faith.

A God who felt lost by God. If the crucifixion teaches us about God's presence, it reveals that God is most present when God feels most absent. I've come to understand that belief is human—but so is doubt. More still, belief and doubt are both divine.

There is another Good Friday story that brings solace during the dark night of the soul. Óscar Romero, a former archbishop of San Salvador, preached these words on Good Friday the year before he was assassinated:

> God is not failing us when we don't feel his presence. Let's not say: God doesn't do what I pray for so much, and therefore I don't pray any more. God exists, and he exists even more, the farther you feel from him. God is closer to you when you think he is farther away and doesn't hear you. When you feel the anguished desire for God to come near because you don't feel him present, then God is very close to your anguish.[1]

I wondered if archbishop Romero believed those words when he wrote them or whether he wrote them because he wanted to believe them. I feared my faith would soon be locked up in a tomb where it couldn't be resuscitated. I prayed for resurrection—a new, glorified, and permanent faith. I could not conjure this faith by my own efforts. It would take an act of God.

If there is a Good Friday for your faith, then there must also be an Easter Sunday, right?

· · · · · · · · · · · · · · · · ✦ · · · · · · · · · · · · · · · ·

The closer you move to God, the closer you must move to the fullness of the human experience. This, of course, will include a deep sense of joy, but it must also include profound pain.

What do you do when the faith you once had starts to disintegrate in your hands?

When romance fades, you double down in commitment or bury the relationship. One of my favorite quotes for at least the last ten years has been one attributed to Martin Luther: "If I knew the world would end tomorrow, I would plant a tree." No one knows if he mouthed those words. It's an optimistic line for a rather pessimistic thinker, which is one reason I want to believe the words left his mouth (all evidence to the contrary).

After all, there's a chance that our world could end tomorrow. Many of us fear at least one of the following: nuclear warfare, a sweltering earth, raging neoliberalism, and dying faith. And so, we must learn to plant bulbs in the fall, just as everything is dying, hoping we'll live to see tulips in spring.

Sometimes, the best way to plant a bulb is by going to work.

Zechariah was my patron saint for an entire year. I met him anew in the Christian season of Advent, the four-week period before Christmas, marked by waiting and yearning for the Christ child's birth. I waited for *Immanuel*, God with us, to be born in my life. For God to be with me.

Zechariah was dealt a difficult hand. He and his wife, Elizabeth, were childless. To say they were righteous and childless would be considered hypocrisy. Other Jews likely thought God was punishing them for their unrighteousness. Zechariah was also a priest of Israel. His job was to go into the temple, deep down into God's home, to burn incense. Did Zechariah feel alone even when he went into God's own heart?

Zechariah is admirable because he kept showing up. Sometimes, that's what hope looks like. Longing does not know any excess. But it also doesn't know any dearth. A sky ripped open sounds great, but most of us just hope for a good night's sleep. A better coworker. That she'll get out of the hospital by Christmas Day. Hope doesn't always have to be so heroic. Sometimes, hope is brushing your teeth and getting dressed the week after the funeral. It's planting a garden when a groundhog destroyed last year's. Hope is buying energy-efficient lightbulbs after the latest climate report has been released. When the world is caving in on itself, we can sit down at the piano and write a song. That's hope, too.

Saint Augustine is credited with saying, "Hope has two beautiful daughters: Anger and Courage. Anger at the way things are, and Courage to see that they do not remain as they are."[2] I also think that Hope has two less attractive, chain-smoking stepdaughters. They're named Duty and Perseverance. Duty to show up today and Perseverance to show up again tomorrow.

God uses people who have just enough hope to show up. It's not bold or heroic; it's the path of least resistance. It's the bare minimum amount of hope—just enough to pass the course, to get the paycheck, to stay out of the hospital. But it's an open door, and God's done more with less. We show up. Not because we want to but because sometimes we must learn to wait. Jesus will be born again, but there's no way to induce him to come earlier than he chooses. In the meantime, we go into the temple and burn incense. We wait.

Something might come when we least expect it. A contraction. It's go time. God is speaking something new into existence. A light is rising against the night sky. And a star is shining. Follow it—all the way to the stable. A Savior will be there. He must be, right? It's our only hope.

Until then, all we can do is show up today.

And then tomorrow.

How does a cactus bloom in the bleakest conditions? I became envious of Jacob, who wrestled with God by the River Jabbock in the dark when all seemed lost (Gen. 32:22–32). As Jacob prayed, a man appeared, grabbed him, and threw him to the ground. We're not told this is God, but we ought not be surprised if it was God. God is the one who promises to show up when everyone else has left. Jacob came to God for solace and comfort, and when he opened his eyes, he slammed against God's skin while his chest was heaving for another breath.

Wrestling is passionate, perseverant, and painful. Most of all, it's intimate. Jacob wrestled with God the entire night, refusing to let go of this man until he received a blessing. "I will not let go, unless you bless me!"

he says. God throws Jacob's hip out of joint with just a slight of the hand, but Jacob refuses to let go.

And then Jacob is blessed. He is called Israel, or "one who wrestles with God." The sun rises as Jacob limps away; he would never walk the same again. Sometimes, a blessing only comes through a bruising. Other times, the blessing is the bruise.

Jacob and all of us who follow in his footsteps are promised a life of wrestling. Sometimes you'll have to wait for God to make good on that promise.

Do you stop praying because you no longer believe in God? Or do you no longer believe in God because you've stopped praying? Recently, I told someone that the desire to pray is probably enough. Because if you have the desire to pray, then you have the desire for God.

God is in the desire.

I wish someone had told me that fifteen years ago.

Around this time, I became acutely aware of how I had been hurt by following God through the church. To live is to receive wounds—even from the very people who love you more than life itself, even from the place that promises to be a sanctuary or a safe place.

My wounds barely broke the skin, and I consider myself lucky. Still, there were altar calls that made me wallow in depravity. A well-meaning pastor gave me a chalice and plate symbolizing the Eucharist when I was most vulnerable, discerning what to do with my life. He said with confidence, "You are called to this." I listened to him, even though I never fully felt God telling me the same message. I tried to tell a board of pastors about my real call to ministry, but they didn't, or couldn't, listen. The very people who claim to represent God make mistakes.

That hurts.

God felt like the cause and cure for my hardship. Johannes de silentio, one of Søren Kierkegaard's pseudonyms, writes, "Isn't it true that those whom God blesses he damns in the same breath?"[3] The kiss of life is a kiss of death. I wondered if my life would have been easier if I had never been introduced to the waters in the first place.

Is there a story that would have hurt less?

I knew that I would never walk away. I am not afraid of the threat of eternal damnation or bogus doctrines like the rapture. My biggest fear was the loss of an identity. Who would I be without this story and these rituals? What would I say when I held my first baby, overwhelmed by the depth of life? What could I proclaim at the graveside of a lost friend? Could I find a better story? I thought about Peter's words to Jesus: "Lord, to whom can we go? You have the words of eternal life" (John 6:68).

Like novelist Julian Barnes, I knew that if I gave up God, I'd miss him.[4] All belief, whether in a god or no god, is fragile and susceptible to doubt.[5]

⸰⸰⸰⸰⸰⸰⸰⸰⸰⸰⸰⸰⸰⸰⸰⸰⸰⸰⸰ ✦ ⸰⸰⸰⸰⸰⸰⸰⸰⸰⸰⸰⸰⸰⸰⸰⸰⸰⸰⸰

Abraham Joshua Heschel, a brilliant rabbi, once defined faith as faithfulness to a time when we had faith. I don't buy it—not entirely. Memory is no substitute for presence. It's not enough to say that Jesus rose from the dead in the past when you need a resurrection in the present.

There will be times when you long to return to Eden, when believing is as effortless as breathing. But you can't reenter the womb, where you were fed and warmed—connected to God with a cord. Every relationship changes, deepens, and becomes strained over time. You move further away from your new birth. The houses you once knew as home will become small and outdated for all your experiences and ideas and relationships. It's hard to breathe. You must wiggle out of your shell and look for something roomier to grow into.

Dietrich Bonhoeffer, a pastor and theologian during the Third Reich, delivered a confirmation sermon to his youth who were learning about the basics of the Christian faith. He told them this important message: Your faith cannot be stored. You cannot put it in a warehouse and rely on it day after day. You can only have enough faith for the day—like manna.

When the Israelites escaped Egypt, God delivered manna, a thin, flaky piece of bread. The Israelites only received enough for the day. If they tried to store it or hoard it, then it would rot. Bonhoeffer told the new Christians that God would give them enough faith for the day—the present. This also means the faith they received yesterday, last month, and last year would not sustain them.[6]

I realize now that I had enough manna—but only enough—to get me through the day.

I held tightly to an old Zen saying: "In the beginning, mountains are mountains and rivers are rivers; later on, mountains are not mountains and rivers are not rivers; and still later, mountains are mountains and rivers are rivers." In other words, if your faith is no longer faith, it can become faith again. That doesn't mean the mountains and rivers will be exactly like they were before.

Some mountains might be taller, others smaller.

Rivers will flow in new directions.

Names might be changed.

Paul Ricoeur says this is your "second naïveté" when you receive the renewed appreciation for life that comes only after being lost and found.[7] And in the process, maybe I was saved from worshipping a God who promised prosperity.

I found the God who promised holiness.

There is a phrase I heard in youth group, "If you feel far away from God, guess who moved?" The answer, of course, is you, the human being; God cannot move. It might be true that God cannot move, but I know God will occasionally hide. I'm not sure why. In the game of divine hide and seek, God becomes cloaked in a baby in a manger, a king on the cross. Maybe God hides so we will learn to look harder. And the longer we look, the more we realize that God will be found in the places where God wants to be found. The hidden God (*Deus absconditus*) will not be controlled by our terms.

In the seeking, faith strengthens and grows.

Feelings are too flimsy to sustain faith. Flannery O'Connor might be right that "faith is what someone knows to be true, whether they believe it or not."[8] We make a mistake when we presume that those baptized into the church have perfect faith. Perfect faith isn't actually faith. The only faith I know is broken and riddled with doubt and insecurity. Some days, it hangs by a thread.

Lauren Winner tells the story of a young girl who is about to be confirmed in the church before she starts having misgivings. "Who in their right mind can believe all these things?" she cried to her father. She was wise to fear a promise that would last the rest of her life.

Her father also responded wisely: "What you promise when you are confirmed is not that you will believe this forever. What you promise when you are confirmed is that this is the story you will wrestle with forever."[9] Like every marriage, your feelings vary, but the promise can always endure. Staying monogamous to one God, one story, feels foolish at times. That's why I affirm my faith weekly—especially when I don't believe it.

An ancient tradition says that the wind didn't move and the water didn't budge when Moses got to the edge of the Red Sea with the Israelites—at least, not at first. Pharaoh and his army were on their heels, but there was no way through the water. One brave Israelite took a step into the sea. There was no path, but he kept walking anyway. He went knee-deep. Waist-deep. The water rose to his neck. Finally, the water began to part when he was submerged completely.

Isn't this what faith is like? God pulls us out of our depth to the place where we can't feel our feet touching the bottom of the ocean floor. We submerge ourselves into the water, all evidence to the contrary, and wait for the wind to blow.

Prayer
Pestered by God

Nothing feels more wasteful than prayer. I mean this sincerely. When my plate gets full, prayer moves down a notch on my to-do list. I push it off to nighttime; then, I'll push it to the morning. Next thing I know, I haven't set aside time for quiet and deliberate prayer in a full month. If you ask me to pray for you, I will. That's because I pray when I'm seen, like a Pharisee on the street corner—devout and pious. What we do in the quiet or the dark, with no one watching, easily falls by the wayside.

Prayer does not come naturally. Like most others, I've tried every prayer gimmick I can find: prayer beads and rosaries, chanted prayer, meditative prayer, and prayer books. I've set reminders on my phone. I've read books about prayer by those who claim to pray, hoping that God would count reading about prayer as a kind of prayer. I've even convinced myself that prayer is not an action but a way of life. When you conflate prayer with attentiveness, you never have to get on your knees, close your eyes, or speak to God. I've learned how to pray without ceasing without ever actually praying.

None of this is novel. It's hard to find any saint who hasn't complained about prayer. Even the most devout followers of God have bowed their heads and started to count tiles, think about grocery lists, or wander off to a more fantastical land.

Mother Teresa of Calcutta, possibly the twentieth century's most widely recognized saint, found prayer difficult for decades. "I utter words of community prayers," she wrote, "and try my utmost to get out of every word the sweetness it has to give—but my prayer of union is not there any longer—I no longer pray."[1] Perhaps the closer you are to God, the more God will feel absent. Some maintain that God withholds consolation so you long for God, not the spiritual feeling. Then, you have the chance to prove that your prayers were never about the feeling in the first place. Prayer becomes an end in itself, or it becomes nothing at all.

I suspect that prayer feels so wasteful because we rarely get evidence that it's worked. We're not *actually* doing anything. Thus, it's a cultural faux pas to offer thoughts and prayers. Prayer is the easiest way to front compassion.

When tornadoes devastated Oklahoma a few years ago, Ricky Gervais tweeted, in response to a note about sending prayers for the victims, "I feel like an idiot now . . . I only sent money."[2] Too many prayers haven't been answered our way: The cancer was not cured, there was no release from some oppression, or the hurricane still hit the coast. You really wanted that parking spot. Even Jesus prayed, "Father, if you are willing, remove this cup from me" (Luke 22:42). And he marched toward the cross.

Do our words go beyond the ceiling? Does prayer change God's mind? Does prayer enable God to do things in our world that would not have happened otherwise? What's the use of telling God what God ought to already know in the first place? And really, what's the use of a God who needs me for advice, anyway? My seven-year-old doesn't even want my advice. Is God that desperate?

There are theological responses to most of these problems. One might say God is always working for the most goodness in every situation, but God sees the whole picture; we see just a piece of the puzzle. Or this: To be loving is to be noncoercive. Maybe there are plenty of things that God can't do; God's power is limited and shaped by God's love.

Ultimately, we don't know why God doesn't always intervene, protect, or restore. Explanations can appease the mind, but they'll rarely satisfy the heart of a grieving widow as she copes with trauma. All we know for sure is that prayer is a great mystery, and we believe that God will make good on the promises that were made.

In the meantime, the best I can do is share a story that Jesus tells the Pharisees. It's a parable that has nothing and everything to do with prayer that's found in Luke 18:1–8.

There's a judge in town. His job is to maintain the peace—to be fair. But he's crooked and biased toward the wealthy. He's quite open that he doesn't like people and doesn't think twice about God's opinion. And he walks past this desperate widow every day. Widows were some of the most vulnerable citizens in the society. Her husband has died, and she has no safety net and nowhere to turn. She is alone, in the streets, desperate for help. And she has a complaint to take up with the judiciary. We don't know her exact problem, but we can make an educated guess: As a woman alone in the first century, the widow was vulnerable to being taken advantage of financially and physically. Her last-ditch effort is to appeal to a judge.

She waits for him on the porch every morning before the office opens. The bailiffs drag her away, but she shows up the next day. Like Martin Luther King Jr. who cried out to the worn-out, bloodied marchers, "How long? How long? . . . How long will it take?"

The judge tries his best to ignore her. He can't. One day, the judge gives in. She's too much. If you look at your Bible, it might say that he gives in because she "keeps bothering" him (Luke 18:5). Here's another translation of the Greek: "She wears me out with continued blows under the eye."

Her relentless pursuit of justice eventually pays off. Here's Jesus's point: If this judge helps the widow, won't God do the same? (Luke 18:7).

If we swarm God like gnats, maybe God will eventually get fed up; God can only swat us away so many times. In Genesis, God loses his temper and is about to destroy Sodom and Gomorrah, but Abraham catches God and talks God down. And they argue like they're trying to get the lowest price at an auction. Another time, God sees that the people he freed from Egypt are creating and worshipping golden calves. God loses it and threatens destruction. Moses grabs God's attention. He asks God to stop and count to ten slowly. God's mind is changed, and the people live.

Should we talk to God like that, too? I've seen a lot of desperate widows—folks going through broken marriages, parents dealing with prodigal children, and others living lives of quiet desperation. Hurricanes have wreaked havoc across the Atlantic, and I rarely pester God about it like this widow. And it's odd because we're an entitled culture. We're used to getting what we want. If a restaurant serves us an overdone steak, we'll send it back (or ask our spouse to do it for us). But we don't dare try that with God. Our world is full of injustices, and we accept it as the norm. That's just the way it is. If we take Scripture seriously, maybe we should not let God off the hook. We should bargain and shout until justice rolls like an ever-flowing stream.

I once heard a story about Mother Teresa visiting a highbrow criminal lawyer—a powerful guy. He owned the Washington Redskins and the Baltimore Orioles. He lawyered for Frank Sinatra and Richard Nixon. He was a big deal. Teresa was raising money for an AIDS hospice, hoping this lawyer would throw a few bucks her way. Before Teresa arrived, this lawyer turned to his buddy and said, "You know, AIDS is not my favorite disease. I don't want to contribute, but I've got this Catholic coming to see me, and I don't know what to do." They agreed to hear her out and then politely turn her away. Teresa arrived. She made her case. The lawyers politely said no.

Teresa said, "Let's pray about it." They bowed their heads.

Teresa then gave her pitch again. The lawyer said, "No."

But Teresa started praying again.

When she said, "Amen," the lawyer looked up to the ceiling and said, "All right, all right, get me my checkbook!" That's persistence.

Jesus ends his parable with an argumentum a fortiori—an argument from greater to lesser. If this God-forsaking judge helps this needy widow, how much more will God hear the requests of us, God's very children? What kind of God do you think you have? An unjust judge, disinterested, with no time to hear your case? A God who's ready to put us behind bars and throw away the key?

God's not that judge. You don't have to show up at five a.m. and bang on the door, knuckles bleeding, every day, all day. God hears you every time you bow your head. The good news is that God already loves us more than we love God. You don't have to coax God into caring about the world.

Earlier in the Gospel, Jesus says, "If you, then, who are evil, know how to give good gifts to your children, how much more will the heavenly Father give the Holy Spirit to those who ask him!" (Luke 11:13).

Madeleine L'Engle writes of the long weekend she and her husband spent waiting for a biopsy result. She kept praying, "Please, dear God, don't let it be cancer." Someone suggested that she was wasting her time. The cancer was already malignant, or it wasn't. But she wrote in her journal, "I can't live with that. I think we can pray." Later, she added,

> Prayer is love, and love is never wasted.... Surely, the prayers have sustained me, are sustaining me. Perhaps there will be unexpected answers to these prayers, answers I may not even be aware of for years. But they are not wasted. They are not lost. I do not know where they have gone, but I believe God holds them, hand outstretched to receive them like precious pearls.[3]

Better yet, God gives us God's own self through the Spirit—freely, generously, compassionately. It might not be what we want—the new car or promotion. Not even perfect health. But God always gives the Holy Spirit. And there we find mercy, forgiveness, peace—salvation. It's enough to sustain us until the day that God will act definitively, defeating sin and death once and for all.

Most of the time, God doesn't need to be convinced to care. The real problem is me. It's probably you, too. An alternate reading of this parable is that it's really about God's persistence. Couldn't it be true that Jesus is the vulnerable widow protesting for justice? We walk right by her in her rags, preoccupied with our schedules, to-dos, and self-importance. We're the unjust judges—the ones keeping score and deliberating about who needs our attention and who doesn't. But God shows up again on our heart's porch, knocking on the door until we pay attention to the needs of our neighbors.

And this is where we discover the heart of prayer: If we make demands of God, God will also make demands on us. It's less about getting what we want and more about listening to what God wants. Perhaps this is the most crucial reason why we pray: Prayer connects us with God and allows us to hear God's voice. God knows what's happening. Do we?

I'm constantly challenged by Martin Luther, who supposedly started a busy day by saying, "I have so much to do today; I shall spend the first three hours in prayer."[4] Smart man. Luther knew that our priorities might change when we start our day in prayer. In prayer, we take stock of our overflowing buckets of thanksgiving, joy, grief, and pain. There's Aunt Kerry, who was just diagnosed with cancer. North Korea points its missiles at Hawaii (or wherever). Your daughter's goldfish passed away. A tragic accident happened in the neighborhood. We empty it into God's hands and pay attention to what overflows into our own. Suddenly, you might drop everything on your agenda and go be with the person who needs your thoughts and prayers.

Does prayer change things? Yes. Prayer changes things, and often, it changes our hearts. Slowly, knock by knock, God will pull back the layers of our hearts, cleaning and scrubbing, forming, and reforming, until we learn to love the world as God loves. Be careful when you pray for something, because God might call you to be the answer.

So don't badger God and expect God not to harass you back. Like an old married couple, we bicker back and forth until someone finally cleans the house and washes the dishes. What will it take for God to finally hear our shouts, "Enough! Enough!" What will it take for us to give in to God's relentless desire for justice? How many times will God have to ask?

The world might look at us like we're wasting time banging on God's door. But we pray because God is knocking on the door of our world. We should answer it if we're courageous enough. God's justice, and ours, depends on it.

Let's waste some time, shall we?

BENEDICTION

Watching the Tides

Worship ought to be as natural and necessary as our breath. Inhaling, however natural, takes work. The diaphragm must contract to create space in the chest cavity for the lungs to expand and receive the air. Exhaling, on the other hand, is mostly effortless. Your body relaxes to push the air out of your system. And so it ought to be in the Christian life. Take a breath. Inhale God's goodness, grace, and peace. Release your breath. Exhale God's goodness, grace, and peace.

No breath is complete without the exhale. When we come into contact with the living breath of the Holy Spirit, we cannot help but exhale it into the world. There is nothing more natural.

Inhale.
Exhale.
Inhale.

. . . . ✝ . . . .

The ultimate test of a church's liturgical life is whether it changes lives. How we leave is at least as important as how we arrive. An experience of God that is self-serving, a religious opiate that numbs you to the pains and problems of the world, is probably not an experience of God. The Greek word for church, *ekklesia*, refers to people called out. Called out of what?

Called out of darkness and into light.

Called out of a building and into the world.

At the end of the service, the pastor stands up with open arms to give a benediction. It's a blessing and a rallying cry to return to a broken world that needs healing. Worship demands action. If saints aren't being made more Christlike, or if chains aren't being broken and powers and principalities aren't vanquished, then it's not a right experience of God. It's just fairy tales and self-help—or worse, entertainment. The taste of the bread and wine must make us hungrier for real life, which is life as God intends in the kingdom of God.

Our lives, like our breath—like the waves—like the people of God,
inhale
in order to exhale.

Many folks wished me rest and relaxation as I packed for a pilgrimage on St. Cuthbert's Way through Scotland and England. I'm not sure they knew we were walking sixty miles. There would be no margaritas on the beach—only foamy, room temperature ales at night to forget about aching feet. Nor did they realize that pilgrimage is not about yelping coffee shops and creating manicured experiences that can be caught in a picture, packaged up, and taken home as a souvenir. Our intention was to walk, inwardly and outwardly, to see and be seen. If we could learn to discern the peace of Christ while ascending a thousand feet walking over rolling hills, then we might learn to find peace in whatever pains and frustrations await us in the future.

The best way I know to describe the difference between vacations and pilgrimages is this: Vacations have checklists; pilgrimages don't. Vacations are about consumption and comfort. Determine what you want from the place and go get it. A day can be full, or it can be empty, depending on what you desire. It's up to you to experience the very best of the place, whether that happens to be a nap on a beautiful beach or a hike up the tallest mountain.

A pilgrimage, on the other hand, is a long, meandering walk following those who have walked before you. There are predetermined beginnings and endings, but the middle is about surprise and interruption. You might not eat at the best restaurant in Edinburgh, but you'll have the freedom to follow a stray sheep into the woods and risk getting lost. There is time to pop into a small Scottish Methodist church in the middle of their Alcoholics Anonymous meeting for a free cupcake and a conversation.

No one penciled that into the day's itinerary. Christ's presence is ubiquitous. Christ must be in the city's best haggis, but Christ is also in a group of nonreligious strangers who found sanctuary in a church with lukewarm coffee and stale cupcakes.

A pilgrimage is a better representation of the lives we actually live.

If you try to treat life like a vacation, you're bound to be disappointed when you don't receive the very best life has to offer. But if you treat life like a pilgrimage, you might stumble into the very something you never knew you wanted. A pilgrimage, like life, doesn't preclude getting lost. It promises it. In those moments when you can't see the path through the trees, you will find God.

After we boarded our flight out of Philadelphia toward Edinburgh, it wasn't long before some of us felt drops of water trickling from the ceiling panel and landing on our heads. The pilot clicked on the intercom to tell us that there was an air conditioning issue. Maybe there was a gaping hole somewhere in the ceiling of the plane. Who's to say? I thought of my baptism, because I am trained to think about my baptism when drops of water fall on my head. Every time we see water, we ought to think about who we are, especially when we are about to be hoisted thousands of feet into the air inside a metal tube.

We deplaned and waited in the terminal for a new aircraft that would transport us to Edinburgh. Our optimistic airline officials told us that we were going to depart at one a.m. One quickly became two. Finally, two-thirty. They told us that we had a fifty-fifty chance of taking off before the three o'clock window closed and the flight would be canceled. The odds were likely closer to thirty-seventy, but the bars had already closed and there was a palpable sense of uprising due to canceled tee times at St. Andrew's, the home of golf.

I put my money on a cheap hotel in Philly, and we rolled the dice.

The new aircraft arrived, but the flight was canceled despite the "valiant" effort by the heroic airline staff. The issue wasn't the engine or other mechanical problems but a flat tire—on an airplane. There was no air. The air, wherever it was blowing, was not blowing us to our intended destination. We were grounded in Philadelphia with meal vouchers that didn't work.

Early Scottish missionaries put themselves in small round boats made of wickerwork, called coracles, and set off to sea praying that the Lord would blow them in the right direction. They had no control over their destination. They cast lots with wind and water with their lives hanging in the balance. Hopefully, they would arrive on land to start their ministries—wherever that happened to be. They relinquished their paddles, trusted the waves of their baptism, and surrendered to the wind of the Spirit. Today's church lacks that kind of courage. It's much easier to pray "Send us, O Lord" and then crank the motor and put your hands on the wheel.

We didn't choose to walk a leg of Cuthbert's Way in Philadelphia, and yet we had no other choice but to pilgrim through national museums and monuments. It's possible we were on the right path, regardless. On the first full day, we walked through downtown Philly and found ourselves on Cuthbert Street. A serendipitous wink from God? Maybe it was a sadistic joke. God might give us what we want, like St. Cuthbert's Way, but it won't always manifest in the ways we imagine.

We walked.

God was in holy meals of cheesesteaks and beer.

We walked.

We ascended the Rocky steps, a shrine for bad eighties movies, and pumped our fists into the sky.

We waited.

One fellow pilgrim reminded me that Celtic monks believed that "it is always better to travel than to arrive. Once we think we have arrived, our souls have died." It's a nice sentiment when you feel like you're headed in the right direction. Not when you're exiled at a gaming convention in Philadelphia's Clarion Hotel. And yet, like it or not, it's true. Christians, and especially Christian pilgrims, know that life can't be controlled. We're always pilgrimaging—somewhere.

The Christian life, insofar as it's a pilgrimage, can be condensed into a labyrinth, a walk with twists and turns and too many switchbacks. We're all one canceled flight, one virus, one mutated cell away from purgatories spent in airports or hospital rooms. Most of us have a sense we're walking in the right direction, but then the trail name suddenly changes, and we realize that a U-turn is in order. Life rarely goes according to plan. Even when it does, there is always the lure of a more attractive path.

Is there a more successful one?

A more faithful one?

One where I'd be happier?

But a labyrinth is not a maze. In a maze, you can get lost, or become anxious that you're not walking in the right direction. In a labyrinth, there is only one path that winds toward the center and one path that winds toward the exit. All you have to do is stay on the path. There is a saying in the Black church that God writes straight with crooked lines. The journey of faith is rarely a direct route, but it will always end in the right place—God's arms. The best you can do is pay attention to the place where each foot lands, always making sure that your heart is pointed toward the heart of God.

• • • • • • • • • • • • • ✦ • • • • • • • • • • • • • •

We arrived in Scotland to walk the rest of Cuthbert's Way two days later than planned. I sometimes wonder if the detour made it more beautiful. Nothing was taken for granted. We walked—we trudged by sheep in fields, then up rolling hills, through gates, and over walls. We had time to start and stop. Feast and fast. Make wrong turns. Find the trail. Begin again. It wasn't always restful, but it was always grace. There was no other way to arrive at our destination.

Our final goal was a monastery on Holy Island, or Lindisfarne, in Northumberland. We reached the shoreline and looked at Holy Island in the distance. We took off our shoes and stepped onto the ocean floor to walk to the island, which can be reached by foot during low tide. The soft ocean mud massaged my blistered feet and thanked us for our walk. I joined with the millions of feet that have crossed through the water that joins us as Christ's body.

St. Cuthbert's priory on Holy Island is unique because it's not always accessible. It's a tidal island. As the North Sea comes in, Lindisfarne is cut off. But when the tide recedes, there is a causeway from the mainland to the island. The tides fall and rise, creating a pattern of access to and prohibition from the island.

The island was a metaphor for St. Cuthbert's life. Cuthbert, a monk, bishop, and hermit, wanted nothing more than to pray in a life of quiet and contemplation, but he kept getting interrupted by the world. The tides moved in, and he receded into quiet contemplation, but the tides moved out, and he was bombarded with noisy visitors and their questions. St. Cuthbert couldn't change the rhythms of the sea, but he shaped a balanced life of solitude and community with the waxing and waning of the waves. The tides pulled him inward.

He inhaled.

They pushed him outward into the world.

He exhaled.

Cuthbert reminds us that we'll never control the tides, but we can pay attention to their movements and discern when and where to walk. The tide rolls in, and we might get stuck in Philadelphia. God will be there, waiting. And when the tide rolls out, God will lead us through the sea into freedom.

I continue to walk the Christian way because Holy Island is always on the horizon. One day, I'll arrive. Until then, I pay attention to the tides. I look for the wind. I put one foot ahead of the other and continue to walk toward freedom. I rarely know where I'm going, but I know of no other way to walk.

My Lord God, I have no idea where I am going. I do not see the road ahead of me. I cannot know for certain where it will end. Nor do I really know myself, and the fact that I think that I am following your will does not mean that I am actually doing so. But I believe that the desire to please you does in fact please you. And I hope I have that desire in all that I am doing. I hope that I will never do anything apart from that desire. And I know that if I do this you will lead me by the right road though I may know nothing about it. Therefore will I trust you always though I may seem to be lost and in the shadow of death. I will not fear, for you are ever with me, and you will never leave me to face my perils alone.

—Thomas Merton[1]

Following God's (Ordinary) Call

I worked at a college whose motto was "You can go anywhere from here." During visitation days, the president stood in front of scared, sometimes eager, and always overwhelmed high school seniors and told them about the institution's famous graduates. There weren't many with great notability—a couple of professional baseball players, a rock star, a CEO or two. The promise was that they could be next in the line of successful graduates. Extraordinary.

With his slicked-back hair and charming southern drawl, the president sounded less like an inspirational speaker and more like a used car salesman. This degree is going to get you fifty miles per gallon. I hated nothing more. The promise of living unbounded with a liberal arts degree was never a reality, and it's becoming more implausible by the year.

Most young people are already overwhelmed by the prospects of finding a good job—and if we're honest, that's not something troubling just teens and twentysomethings these days. They're supposed to grab the bull by the horns (bad advice because that animal is four times their size) and go anywhere. How does someone locate anywhere? What if anywhere is not at the top of the ladder, in the biggest bank account, or on a field with the most spectators? What if anywhere is actually an elementary school in a small rural town where they spend their time wiping runny noses?

It's almost impossible to find a map to anywhere when you are threatened by everywhere. Søren Kierkegaard put it even more succinctly: "Anxiety is the dizziness of freedom."[1] He means that anxiety is living in a world where we are told we can be anything. Choice is good, but too much choice leads to counselors and SSRIs.

This is why choosing a restaurant when you're on vacation is so difficult. How do you choose where to eat with so many different options? You've got to know all about James Beard and Michelin Stars without forgetting that the locals prefer underground spots that are undiscoverable by tourists. You only get one shot at this. Fire up Yelp, scroll through the options, and hope you don't miss out on the best meal of your life.

Now imagine that you're choosing the one meal you will eat for the rest of your life.

That's called vertigo.

"One would have no anxiety if there were no possibility whatsoever," writes Kierkegaard.[2] But there is possibility, and it's the possibility that makes us human—we alone have the possibility to pursue a specific life, seek a particular adventure, and choose among endless avenues. You can take personal inventories, strengths finders, and career quizzes to ease the burden of choosing anywhere. Eventually though, you must take a leap of faith and apply for a job. And until you make that choice, there will be paralysis or a desire to pursue graduate school (endlessly). At worst, there will be existential despair (conscious or unconscious), a sickness in your spirit, or a constant fear of missing out.

What is it that you want?

Most people throughout the history of the world would think this dilemma is absurd. When I was young, I googled my last name and discovered that "Snider" is a variation of a German and Jewish word that means *tailor*. I wondered if I would have been a tailor had I been born five hundred years ago. I imagined a little shop on the corner of the street that said "Schneider's." Having learned the work from his father, my father would teach me the trade that I would teach my children. I wondered if my people were less anxious when they knew they would spend their lives with needles and thread, hand stitching garments to clothe their neighbors. We all would have held hands as we died a devastating death of the black plague.

Today, we are blessed and cursed with dreams. For the rest of your life, people will ask you, "What do you do?" The question of identity is always lingering beneath the surface of vocation. They don't really care about your work; they want to know who you are.

・・・・・・・・・・・・・✦・・・・・・・・・・・・・

In a world where I could be anything, I didn't shoot for the stars or giant sequoias. Instead, I aimed for the humanities. I was told to follow my dreams until they realized I dreamt about the medieval church and papacy. Are you sure that you can't dream again? You know you'll never make any money with a religion and philosophy degree, right? No, I have never heard that before. Thanks.

On my healthy days, I accept the fact that I love to play with words and pictures. Blood is gross, and I'd rather ask about the meaning of math than solve math problems. Plus, humanity degrees are increasingly rare, on a trajectory toward extinction, making them more valuable. I'm a diamond in an imitative pile of STEM degrees. The ancient Greeks used to think that becoming a full, thoughtful person was the highest good. Not everything has to be instrumentalized to a financial end.

Still, their warnings were not wrong—there really isn't much to do with a humanities degree. One still has to find work that the world deems worthy of compensation. Unable to secure payment to read in coffee shops, I set off to make the most rational choice possible. That happened to be pastoring a church. The pastorate was never on my short-list of childhood dreams. Still, the addends of interest, education, and opportunity equaled a sum, which, in my case, was preaching and hospital visits. Reading theology was the gateway to seminary, which was the gateway to preaching, which happened to be the gateway to pastoring. I set out to think about God and became entrusted with souls in the process.

Some days, I think I ended up as a pastor by mistake, though it's not politically correct to say that pastoring is something you choose. Properly speaking, the pastorate is a vocation. The word vocation is rooted in the

Latin *vox* or "voice" and *vocatio,* which means "calling." Vocation is a calling, or something you've heard, as opposed to something you've arbitrarily chosen for yourself. Somehow, pastoring finds you like a stalker who won't leave you alone. Try your best to ignore it, but it will always find an entrance into your house.

There's a sense in the Christian life that we might be called to do work that we would never choose for ourselves—no matter how much soul-searching we do. It's hard to find any biblical characters who chose their jobs after meeting with a career counselor. Moses didn't decide to lead the Israelites out of slavery after pairing his Myers-Briggs with his StrengthsFinder. And Jonah, who was called to preach to the Ninevites, didn't have access to Frederick Buechner's maxim: "Vocation is the place where your greatest gladness meets the world's deep need."[3] God didn't let him follow his great gladness, because there was a deep need. He tried to run away, but God spat him up on the shore of Nineveh and started transforming his gladness.

In seminary, I met many people like these biblical characters; they heard God's voice loud and clear. They could point to a day and time and minute and second where they heard a voice—that I presume sounded like James Earl Jones or Morgan Freeman—calling them to some particular kind of work. Worse yet, many of them knew they would be pastors as early as middle school. My biggest concern in middle school was finding a way to sneak in episodes of *South Park* when my parents went to bed.

I found these people deeply annoying. They were annoying, of course, because I had no idea what to do with my life. Often, our biggest pet peeves usually reveal something about our insecurities or jealousies. Did God lose my number? Or did I hear and ignore the message? Maybe my patron saint was Elijah, who had to listen for a still, small voice barely audible over the noise of the earthquake, wind, and fire.

It's challenging work to discern God's voice. Thomas Aquinas said, "God can do nothing but give you the desire." It's a nice sentiment, but Aquinas never peered into my heart to look at all my competing desires. God's voice is just one cricket chirp in an orchestra of droning. Saint Augustine says we are so bent inward that we can't even desire the things that will bring us life. That strikes me as right. Have you ever wanted something so bad that you convinced yourself it must be God's will that you have it? Have you ever been so sure God was calling you to do something only to realize later that those were your plans, not God's? This explains why God always calls pastors to work at churches in hipster mountain cities or quaint beach towns. Rarely do I hear folks with a hankering to plant a church in rural Appalachia.

We easily confuse Jesus's voice with louder, sexier, and more assertive voices internalized from other places. Is this the Good Shepherd? Or is it a wolf in a sheep's skin? We easily confuse Jesus's voice with the other voices around us. You might think you've differentiated the two, but then someone will tell you that your Jesus sounds a lot like Sean Hannity or Rachel Maddow. They're probably not wrong. That voice you hear inside your head, critiquing, belittling, shaming, and telling you what to do with your life? That's not Jesus. It might be your dad or your mom. Your second-grade teacher, even. Most of the time, it's the market. But it's not Jesus.

Regardless, the voice I heard most clearly was calling me to be a pastor. In most mainline denominations, pastors must defend their case to enter the pastorate through ordination exams. Typically, you are asked to write a long paper and submit sermons and Bible studies. The denominational officials call you in and talk to you about God, spirituality, and theology. It's like a holy version of hazing. You must tell them what you believe but not what you really believe. There's a fine line between saying enough and saying you're a universalist who thinks hell is metaphysically impossible. Here's a helpful line: it's a mystery.

During an ordination interview, you will undoubtedly get asked about your call to ministry. They'll want to know when God called you, how God called you, and how you know it's authentic. You need dates and times with appropriate references that can vouch for your authenticity. Tell your stories with tears if you can. Finally, they want you to say, "God has called me to the ministry, and I'm certain, without a doubt, that this thing is the thing I'm supposed to do with my life, and I'm going to follow God's call wherever it sends me, however much it hurts, for however long it takes, and I'll do it forever or until I can no longer speak."

I said the words while wondering if God and I played a bad game of telephone. God's original message passed through school, mentors, teachers, or my brother who preceded me in ministry. When my calling got to the end of the line, I only heard a muffled voice through a children's walkie-talkie. It was the best I had at the time.

I've since learned that quite a few pastors will repeat the words, "God called me to be a pastor," while also thinking, "It might be fun to brew beer for a living."

Some of them have gone on to minister to folks by brewing beer.

· · · · · · · · · · · · · · · ✦ · · · · · · · · · · · · · · ·

I worried about my calling for the first three years of my ministry until I read *East of Eden* by John Steinbeck. In one of the novel's climactic moments, Lee, a cook and housekeeper, discovers the word *timshel* while reading the story of Cain and Abel in the Scriptures. Throughout the Scriptures, he notices that the word is translated as a command—"thou shalt" or "do thou." We live our lives as an order or promise from God. But, dissatisfied with the definition, Lee continues to research the translation, discovering that the word has been mistranslated. The gold from his mining is "thou mayest." Thou mayest is an open rather than a closed door. You are not at the mercy of fate or circumstance. Instead, at any moment, you may or you may not. But the choice is always yours.

Too often, we interpret vocation as "do thou" and throw ourselves into work as a matter of duty. The call of God is a burden we will bear whether we like it or not; we are obedient. Alternatively, we feel the weight of "thou shalt," a predestination into a life we would never choose for ourselves. No matter what you do, you can not interfere with God's plan for your life. How much of our martyrdom is self-imposed? We'd rather cling to duty and die than find the courage to make a choice and live.

Maybe the truth is that we've mistranslated the most important word of the novel—thou mayest. Hebrew scholars maintain that Steinbeck got the translation wrong, but I believe he got the theology right. Steinbeck writes, "It is easy out of laziness, out of weakness, to throw oneself into the lap of deity, saying, 'I couldn't help it; the way was set.' But think of the glory of the choice! That makes a [hu]man a [hu]man."[4]

I've since stopped worrying about obeying God's perfect calling. I have enough anxiety as it is. Maybe there is not one particular thing that thou shalt do with a life. God doesn't have perfect plans as much as God has purposes for our lives. It's good to have a plan, but plans change. Plans can be an idol that distracts us from the voice of God that never stops calling out to us to make turns and U-turns.

It's much healthier to have a purpose. Your purpose, if we can call it that, is to glorify God—to look like Jesus. That's it. And you can glorify God behind a pulpit, on a playground, or in an office, school, or field. What you decide to do for a living matters less than how the work can be folded into a larger narrative of how God is redeeming, sustaining, and transforming the world. In other words, in a world where you can be anything,

you may pastor. Or,

you may brew beer,

as long as the work helps you love your neighbor and ushers in the kingdom of God.

God gives us the freedom to go anywhere, and it's easier to go anywhere when you believe that Jesus is everywhere.

Most agree that work ought to bring some purpose. Barbara Brown Taylor says that too many of us work jobs that are too small for us.[5] The church is good at romanticizing work that is menial and dehumanizing. We can be complicit in some of the evils of the economy, especially degrading work. We tend to say that you ought to do your job for the glory of God. That's easier to do when you have a multitude of choices and a steady stream of income. It's more complicated when you work on the factory line, behind the cash register, or in the delivery truck. All the while, you're worried about getting food on the table and having enough time and energy to parent your children well.

Everyone I know wants to be compensated fairly for their work, to have their giftedness acknowledged and utilized, and to contribute to something bigger than themselves. Not everyone gets this opportunity. Too many of us are cogs in a wheel we don't get to steer. That's why the Christian vocation is such good news. It reminds us that every person is beloved and worthy of purpose. We get to follow Jesus. What in life is more important than that? Almost regardless of its nature, work can be infinitely meaningful when it's soaked in the waters of our baptism. When it's not, the church must rise and critique all labor that turns human beings into commodities.

For the first few years of my daughter's life, I stayed at home—to serve a vocation and calling as a father. Many days, I longed to accomplish more than changing dirty diapers. Parenting full-time can feel beneath the kind of person who has just graduated with *summa cum laude* distinctions. Worse, domestic work is often slighted, especially for men. A former supervisor told me, "You can't be pastor of First Church if you spend your time with babies." No, it doesn't matter that you know every word of *Goodnight Moon* and *The Little Mouse, the Red Ripe Strawberry, and the Big Hungry Bear*. You're squandering your gifts!

The church has forgotten that Mother Mary had one of the greatest vocations of all time—motherhood, caring for God incarnate. No work was more important.

A popular Christian author's wife was once asked by some pretentious academic at a dinner party what she did for work. "And what is it that *you* do, my dear?" she asked condescendingly.

This mother of two, quick on her feet, said, "I am socializing two Homo sapiens into the dominant values of the Judeo-Christian tradition in order that they might be instruments for the transformation of the social order into the kind of eschatological utopia that God willed from the beginning of creation!"

Then she asked the other person, "And what is it that *you* do?"

I'm just a sociologist.[6]

You can be ordinary. Does that relieve some anxiety?

I first heard it from a bigwig professor—one of the world's preeminent scholars on the Cappadocian Fathers and Saint Augustine. He stood before us, arrogant first-year divinity school students, and said something like this: I have written ten books, or whatever, but ultimately it doesn't matter.

In two or three generations, I will be forgotten. What matters is not what I've written or accomplished but how much I have loved God.

What a relief.

We thought we enrolled in seminary to make some accomplishments in the church tradition, and he told us that we enrolled in seminary to learn how to love God. If we took his advice seriously, we'd save a lot of time of needless striving and acquiring. Thomas Merton said we can spend our whole lives climbing this ladder of success. We finally get to the top, look around, and realize the ladder has been leaning against the wrong wall.

Saint Augustine recalls a day when he stumbled into a drunk man who was overwhelmingly happy. It irked Augustine because he was a tenured professor in Milan with a big house, servants, and world renown. He had everything he was supposed to have. He was rich. He was unhappy.

Conversely, the drunkard on the road had nothing, but somehow, he had attained more. They both found external solutions to cure an internal problem, and a bottle of booze is significantly cheaper than a lifetime's struggle for outward praise.[7] Augustine began to realize that his life would be empty unless he used it for something bigger than himself—for love, for the kingdom, for God.

In that sense, what you do matters less than how you do it. All you need is the desire to follow the one who calls out to you. If the disciples are any indication, there are no qualifications for following Jesus. The opposite is true. Jesus's first followers were often unskilled laborers, working menial jobs. Their sights were set just low enough to see the one calling to them from the shoreline.

Jesus was a big waste of potential. He left the heavenly throne to work as a carpenter and teacher of twelve bumbling students. He forsook the degree, the tenured job with the publications, the Fortune 500 company. It was a pay cut that led to his death. He never quite lived up to his surname, "The Christ," the expectation to overturn the evil powers of the world with force and power. Instead, the cross was his throne. His broken body bore witness to his teaching that the only way to ascend in this life is to descend.

I read what Paul wrote to his friends in Corinth when I need to be reminded of this: "Take a good look, friends, at who you were when you got called into this life. I don't see many of 'the brightest and the best' among you, not many influential, not many from high-society families. Isn't it obvious that God deliberately chose men and women that the culture overlooks and exploits and abuses, chose these 'nobodies' to expose the hollow pretensions of the 'somebodies'?" (1 Cor. 1:26–29 *The Message*).

Is this not just a long, drawn-out way of calling his friends losers? Paul uses a lovely Greek word, *moria,* to describe those who follow that kind of Christ. It's the foundation for our word *moron*. It's hard to tell what Paul is thinking. Is he proposing that those of us who follow a crucified God are morons? Most likely. The Christian tradition is chock-full of wasted potential. You can sign up to follow Jesus right now and get hired. He won't even make you lie about your strengths and weaknesses. As Flannery O'Connor (possibly) said, "You shall know the truth, and the truth will make you odd."

When I traveled to the Holy Land, I met a delightful monk at Jacob's Well, now in an Eastern Orthodox church in the West Bank of Palestine. In the Scriptures, Jesus traveled out of his way to Jacob's Well, where he had no business, to stumble upon people with whom he had no business. There, at the well, he met a woman who was thirsty. Jesus told her, "Everyone who drinks this water will get thirsty again and again. Anyone who drinks the water I give will never thirst—not ever. The water I give will be an artesian spring within, gushing fountains of endless life" (John 4:13–14 *The Message*).

We live in a world with voices that tell us which well we should drink from—who we should be, what we should look like, where to spend our money. That water rarely satisfies. The monastic tradition is one of the last vestiges of those who dare to subvert the lure of worldly comfort and success.[8] Richard Foster notes that monks (and nuns) are the only ones left who are willing to forsake everything we're told that will save us—money, sex, and power. And they exchange it for the one thing that can't be taken away—Jesus, the water of life.

Nuns and monks remind us that a holy life can't be forced into any coherent worldview except the one that begins in a manger and ends with a cross and resurrection.[9] The monk at Jacob's Well sits near the well and dips water for tourists all day. His life is simple: prayer, service, conversation. All he needs is a set of clothing, maybe a Bible, and some arm strength to lower, dip, and raise the basket. He drinks living water. In return, all his thirst is quenched. His life is a descent into the well of Christ. He emerges born again. Every day is a reminder of his baptism.

When you die and rise with Christ, your life is given away to a story you can never completely control. You certainly don't know where God will call you, lead you, or drag you kicking and screaming. But you'll always know who you are. During moments of confusion and anxiety, it is said that Martin Luther would hold his hand to his forehead and repeat to himself, "Martin, be calm; you are baptized." Your life is not wild and precious by your own choices so much as by the God who has drowned you and raised you as a beloved. Everything else will (eventually and prayerfully) fall into place. And when you come to the end, you'll realize you've been at the beginning the whole time—swimming in the river of God's grace, claimed as God's child.

Planted in New Soil

Church doesn't always work as intended. Many churches are cold and individualistic—more exclusive than country clubs. Please, don't act shocked. We have a dark history of exclusion where there was supposed to be embrace. Since its inception, the church has excluded "the other" based on every identity marker imaginable: gender, skin color, religion, sexuality, and ethnicity. During the Crusades, the church created enemies and sought to extinguish them through genocide and ethnic cleansing. Thousands were put to death under the guise of "witch hunts." The Inquisition began the expulsion of Jews and Muslims. Europeans stole men and women with dark skin from their homes, families, and land to force them to work on plantations to build their capital. Christians were quick to take arms with Hitler in the Third Reich.

Most recently, the problem is sexual identity.

And God's heart breaks every time.

The world looks at the church, at us, and calls us hypocrites. And they're right. I'm often tempted to write off the church, too. The apple falls too far from the tree. It's easy to take cheap shots when Christians fail, but that doesn't mean we can't acknowledge the beauty and magnitude of the calling. There will always be a gap between the church and the One they worship. G. K. Chesterton said, "The Christian ideal has not been tried and found wanting. It has been found difficult and left untried."[1] It's not that Christianity is depraved; it's that God is working with people like us—sinners. The odds are stacked against God. Yet God seeks the church until it names the ways it has gone astray, seeks penance, and receives restoration.

Human nature is deeply entrenched in *xenophobia*, or fear of the other. In its mildest form, we merely prefer the people who look like us, smell like us, or pray like us (and, of course, people who vote like us). But in our deepest fear, we exclude and oppress those people. Fear is helpful when a tiger is lurking in the jungle. It's less useful when a Muslim is boarding a plane or a Syrian is looking for refuge. Even today, these biological instincts keep us alive, but they don't always do the same for the harmless stranger looking for safety.

Who is the "other" in your culture, your life, your community? The poor who are hungry in spirit and body. The college student who lives in the interim. The addict, the mentally ill, the one on the street corner with no roof or bed to call home. The one with the different skin color, accent, or smell. People with disabilities who defy your expectations. The immigrant working in construction or the CEO who drives a BMW. The refugee who is too dangerous to welcome into the neighborhood. The political other. The imprisoned and those shackled by hatred. The elderly who are cast out into nursing homes where they neither see nor are seen.

The people that Jesus called friends.

The paradox is that Christians have also been consistently hospitable; they gave rise to the institutions that provide sanctuary to strangers and enemies: hospitals, hospices, and hostels. Emperor Julian, in the year 362, wanted to revive and revitalize the principles of Rome and the beliefs of the Hellenistic faith and culture and thought copying Christian hospitality would help. Julian told his high priest this: "Why do we not observe that it is their benevolence to strangers, their care for the graves of the dead and the pretended holiness of their lives that have done most to increase [Christianity]?" He went on, "For it is disgraceful that when no Jew ever has to beg, and the impious Galileans [Christians] support not only their own poor but ours as well, all men see that our people lack aid from us."[2]

Still today, the most generous people in my life have also been Christians—they are the ones who intrude into my home with casseroles and conversations so intimate I regret them the following day. *Philoxenia*, or love of the stranger, is not natural. Left to our own devices, I'm not sure we'd make the effort. I have yet to find another story that challenges me to join the stranger. And that's one reason I keep showing up on Sunday mornings: I'm forced into relationships I'd never cultivate on my own.

⁘⁘⁘⁘⁘⁘⁘⁘⁘⁘⁘⁘⁘✦⁘⁘⁘⁘⁘⁘⁘⁘⁘⁘⁘⁘⁘

After I graduated from seminary, the bishop sent me to pastor a small congregation in rural Appalachia. I had an affinity for mountains and mountainy things—you know, hiking, kayaking, IPAs, and the kind of people who smoke weed. I soon realized that the people who do mountainy things often differ from those who live and die in the mountains. It turns out that native mountain people don't shop at REI or wear Patagonia. Ironically, they wear Carhartt for its intended purpose, repairing cattle fences, not going to the coffee shop for a Bible study on Romans.

This was a wake-up call, a realization that people are not characters in my story. A geographical area is just a space until you learn it has a story, and it's then that it becomes a place. Like a person, a place must be loved for what it is and not what you want it to be. There is history and memory. Identities have been established across generations—people who have shaped the place and been shaped by it. And it takes time to learn the rhythms of the place—when the dogwoods should bloom or when it's safe to stick a tomato plant in the ground. Unless it's your place, you have much listening to do.

Appalachians, for instance, get a bad rap for being inhospitable. The story goes that years of physical isolation is a recipe for deep family bonds and a distrust of outsiders. That's true—to some extent. Many of my Appalachian parishioners would rather die in a ditch alone than ask a stranger to pull them out. They were quick to make remarks about the influx of Florida tags as they mourned the death of their slow, simple way of life. It's also true that these people will drop off a truckload of firewood when you don't ask for it. Anyway, don't we all get a little worried that Florida might discover and ruin the good thing we have goin'?

My first parishioners were different from me in almost every conceivable way—age, theological beliefs, political affiliation, education level, hobbies, and so on. They collected guns when I never held one. I quoted Barth and Bonhoeffer in my sermons, but they showed up to Bible study with the latest by David Jeremiah. I follow Duke basketball, and they didn't care about basketball (God forgive them).

We held one thing in common, which happened to be the most important thing of all: Jesus. They loved and followed him, and I tried to do the same. Jesus is enough material to construct a family and friendship.

This small church had an excellent record of receiving young pastors from seminary. "We train young preachers," said the church council chairman. "Stick with us, and you might become a bishop one day." They weren't wrong. Their former pastors climbed the ecclesiastical ladder into bigger churches—though not necessarily better ones.

Often, the small church's job in God's great economy of salvation is to break in new pastors the same way horse trainers break in new livestock.[3] The wall in their fellowship hall is lined with young, bright-eyed preachers who came bucking out of seminary ready to create the parishioners in their own image: They'd teach them about Social Trinitarianism and yank the flag out of the sanctuary without even explaining the phrase "Christian nationalism." Other new preachers came shaking, nervous to speak, and unable to preach a sermon. But the parishioners listened attentively even when you plagiarized one-third of your message and your eyes never looked up from the manuscript. At this church, young preachers learned about grace, gained confidence, and left with the skills to run an administrative council meeting and hold a proper funeral. We started as preachers (proclaimers) but left as pastors (shepherds).

When my wife and I moved into the parsonage on our first day, we noticed two mason jars on the front porch. One was large, full of brown liquid, with a big chunk of apple. The other was small and clear, with a skull and crossbones drawn on the side with a Sharpie.

"Oh, God. Is this moonshine?"

"That's not helping the stereotype," I told my wife.

I didn't know what to do with the stuff. I could pour the apple 'shine into a glass and take a big swig. I knew it would burn a little going down. Maybe I would deposit it in a pantry, deep behind expired cans of soup. It's different. Dangerous, even. Or I'd sip the stuff—just once. Then it would be relegated to my top shelf, neither in nor out of sight. That's the way we deal with difference, right? Consumption, exclusion, or tolerance.

A tag attached to the bottles said this: "Just make sure to visit us."

And I made the mental promise that I would. I'd partake of the 'shine with the community that wanted to celebrate and needed to mourn. Strangers aren't meant to be consumed, excluded, or tolerated—they are to be embraced.

※ ※ ※

Every first house visit filled me with a tinge of anxiety. What is it that makes us sit on pins and needles in the presence of a stranger? Maybe it's the obligatory small talk, knowing there is a good chance the conversation will bomb. Have you ever wanted to leave a dinner party or ask your guests to leave but didn't know how to make the first move? That's what it's like to make a house visit in a country church. It's an introvert's worst nightmare. You've been attentive for two hours, but now your eyes are drooping. You're nodding and smiling like the Joker because you don't have enough energy to further the conversation.

Plus, it's never completely safe, is it? There's always a chance that the person is some kind of axe murderer—you'll be the victim of the next true crime phenomenon. It's unlikely. It's more likely that you will die of awkward silence, sipping your bottomless glass of sweet tea while soap operas blare in the background ("I still love you, Laura!").

One of my first visits was to an older man's tiny house two miles down the road. Every first-time visit, I ask the usual: Who are you? Who do you love? Why the church? Tell me a story.

I wasn't prepared for a half-hour conversation about a man named Cooter. To my credit, I didn't laugh a single time. I was a pastor, now—mature. But Jack rarely wanted to talk about anything other than his wife, Jackie. They were the first couple married in the church's sanctuary. They had to "walk the plank" to get out of the sanctuary because the stairs weren't completed. Now she has chronic obstructive pulmonary disease (COPD). She spent most of the day resting in her bedroom while her breathing machine pumped air into her lungs—a metronome of life and death.

Jack was the kind of man who had worked with machines his whole life. His hands were rough and calloused; I thought they could crack and start bleeding when I shook them. But when Jackie got sick, he started wearing an apron around the house, learning domesticity from scratch. His niece taught him how to load the washing machine and fold the clothes. He progressed to following recipes, then cooking; finally, he became somewhat of a chef. When I got to him, he had his own strand of kombucha fermenting in the fridge.

"Jack," I said, "I thought kombucha was for hippies."

He laughed: "Hippies just drink it because they all have IBS from the vegan food."

When I left that afternoon, he shared the potato recipe he promised would make me "slap my granny" (that's Appalachian for damn good—and they are so damn good that my kids ask me to make them weekly). Then he sent me home with the potatoes from his garden.

No one said that rough hands can't be gentle. Jack worked hard at domesticity because he loved hard.

Jack lent my wife and me a field for our first garden that summer. I'm unsure whether he was more excited about teaching us gardening or learning how we'd handle the adversity from aphids. Jack drove us to the feed and seed store and bought our seed. He put me on his tractor, which must have been from the 1970s, and told me to figure it out. I bumped down the road as a line of cars formed behind me. He didn't laugh a single time. But I could tell by the smirk on his face that he enjoyed every minute.

Jack showed me how to till the ground and break up the dirt. I learned how to connect the water pump to the stream in the corner of the field. Finally, we put the seeds in the dirt and formed a burial mound to sprout new life. I listened carefully, learning how to care for a seed in a soil that wasn't my own. Our time together in the garden constructed a renewing of the mind, a way of giving and receiving life, nurturing and protecting new relationships. I wonder if those who spend time in the dirt instinctively know something about hospitality. As Henri Nouwen says, "We create space not to change people, but to offer a space where change can take place."[4]

Gardening is a quintessential lesson in hospitality. The black soil of the earth welcomes seeds with courses of sunlight and water to drink; the seeds settle into their chairs, spring out some roots, and hang out for a while. There is embrace. The soil opens itself up to something other than itself but does not consume the object. Instead, it welcomes the seed with arms open. In the waiting, the seed has the time and space to respond to the soil. If there is good hospitality, the seed will open itself to embrace the soil's nutrients and come into itself—it thrives. In the relationship between the earth and seed, one does not overshadow or absorb the other but rather helps the other flourish. Finally, the soil and the seed will let each other go, having been enriched by the other. The product of hospitality is delicious.

Gardening, then, is theological at its core. I had a professor who challenged his students to produce the first images of God in Scripture. Isn't "gardener" one of the very first images we are given of God? Creation, Eden, literally means the Garden of Delight. "Hear it again," he would say. "God, the gardener. What comes to your mind? What do you see? What do you smell?"[5] God is not distant. God is watering, feeding, weeding, and pruning. God's hands are always in the soil, protecting and enjoying what has been created. Don't you enjoy imagining God overjoyed when a new squash plant turns up by accident? A God who gets pissed off at groundhogs and deer and other rodents but is too generous to exclude them from the garden? A gardening God celebrates each birth and mourns every death.

God has welcomed you into God's garden. God will do whatever it takes for you to flourish.

A man steeped in the dirt knows how to be steeped in the life of another. Jack's life was slow and deliberate, oriented to all that was under his care with attention, gentleness, and responsibility. In most relationships, we put our roots in a vase of water, always ready to pull them up and replant them elsewhere. Jack helped me put my roots deep into the soil, where I could grow and bloom to my fullest potential. You do not have to fear the other when you know the other can nurture life. In God's economy, the weapons used to fend off strangers are bent and molded into gardening tools to nurture perfect welcome.

Sometimes you will feel like the other—you are the stranger who doesn't know the seasons or what the dirt feels like between your fingers or how to plant and harvest. And you have nothing to offer but presence. Luckily, Christian hospitality accepts you as you are without assessment of your utility or anticipation of economic exchange. You are accepted, welcomed, and loved as a child of God. There is no *other* with God. We only have Jesus, the primordial gardener, and those who call him friend. When we come close to Jesus, we are planted together—especially in the soil we'd most like to avoid.

Two years into our relationship, Jack called me in the middle of the night: His wife, Jackie, had been going in and out of consciousness. Jackie had been in at-home hospice care for quite a while; it was a matter of time until her airway was too constricted for her breath to flow in and out. I threw on clothes and went over as quickly as I could. Jackie's immediate family gathered around her bed as she passed from life to death and back into life.

I picked up Jackie's Bible and read her favorite passages as she breathed in short bursts, grabbing whatever air she could hold. When her breathing slowed and her mouth hung open, we pushed a wet sponge in her mouth to keep it from drying out. Jesus was hanging on the cross as a sponge of wine was hoisted up to his mouth.

During one of Jackie's last moments of consciousness, she asked me to keep praying as she gently closed her eyes. We cried and hugged and hoped God would make good on all of God's promises. "Into your hands," I prayed, "we commend Jackie in the sure and certain hope that, together with all who have died in Christ, she will rise with him."

Life is hard and unfair; the horror of death is too much for almost everyone to bear. But Jack had taught me the language of the garden. There, in the garden, we pick up our tools and learn how to welcome life and death. The garden is a bed for death. Maybe the soil is acidic and does not sustain life. Or slugs and parasites have infested the network. Deer, rabbits, and other rodents have stripped the garden of every leaf and bloom. Creation is both beautiful and flawed. The soil is unsafe, yet it produces ripe tomatoes and cucumbers. It's cognitive dissonance.

But God never took off the gloves, nor did God put down the trowel and shears. Instead, God entered the garden to recultivate the soil—God continues to pull weeds, prune, fertilize, and compost death into life. One day, even further down the road, this plant will bear some kind of fruit. The fruit will make its way to our dinner table, where we will celebrate the goodness of life with friends.

When Mary cries at the tomb after Jesus's death, she mistakes Jesus for the gardener. Is it a mistake? Maybe not. Easter begins in a garden, where every end is a bridge to new life. The garden is not where Jesus has died but where Jesus lives today—inviting us into an eternal paradise of pleasure. Christ's resurrection is the eighth day of creation, the day when death no longer reigns.

The beginning and end of our lives depend on the extravagant hospitality of a God who will never stop making room. We return our bodies to the soil, but Christ knows how to work with the dirt. All God needs is a seed. One day, God will kiss the dirt, and all life will rise.

> *The seed is in the ground.*
> *Now may we rest in hope*
> *While darkness does its work.*
> —Wendell Berry[6]

Epilogue
Sending Forth

Every entrance has an exit. Life has forward momentum. This is often good news: You will not be suspended in any one place indefinitely, though many stages of life overstay their welcome. You might feel trapped in a minute that feels like an hour or month or year. It will pass. I've never met an entrance that didn't lead to an exit. Soon, a new door will open. This can be true in even the worst circumstances. If you've ever been with someone in tremendous pain or watched labored breathing persist for weeks, you'll know that even death, the final exit, can be a great emancipator. Before you know it, you'll leave the tomb or rise from the grave to a new way of being and living. You will carry with you the marks of your stay—the scars of happiness and pain.

The bad news is that most endings feel premature. Others are actually premature. Vacations end, the streetlights flip on, the cancer returns, and it's time to come home. The book is slammed shut, and the story ends when the characters still have plenty of life left to live. Some people get more chapters than others. Villains, especially, seem to get the longest storylines, while many of our best protagonists exit sooner than they should. None of this seems fair. Death is not a natural part of the kingdom of God. Almost everyone I know wants to pull God aside for a little chat about how God is running things down here. And God better not give us any platitudes about a vacancy for another angel in heaven.

How do you live when you know the grim reaper is waiting to surprise you and the ones you love the most? That seems to be the most important question that almost everyone is afraid to ask. And yet, we must live with death creeping around every corner, abolishing everything true, good, and beautiful. It's better to become acquainted with death as soon as possible instead of meeting it for the first time as you take your last breath. Death will always be an enemy, but you're better off if it's not a stranger. Keep your friends close and your enemies closer.

· · · · · · · · · · · · · · · · · ✦ · · · · · · · · · · · · · · · · ·

Moses takes his last breath when he is only a few feet away from the land promised to and claimed by Abram and Sarai, lost by the Israelites, and re-promised to him and the Israelites enslaved in Egypt. Can you imagine the nerve?

After forty years of wandering in the wilderness, Moses is a strong 120-year-old man whose knees don't wobble as he takes his final steps up Mount Tabor. He doesn't squint to make out the new home for his people. Scripture even says Moses was full of vigor, which had more to do with sexual strength than physical strength (no need for Viagra, in other words). Moses has one more task: walk down the mountain.

That's when the Lord says to him, "This is the land of which I swore to Abraham . . . . I have let you see it with your eyes, but you shall not cross over there" (Deut. 34:4).

Moses was the child rescued by Pharaoh's daughter while floating down the Nile in a woven basket to escape infanticide. God raised him and spoke to him through a burning bush. He freed his people through the Red Sea and entered the long wilderness journey where he received the Ten Commandments on top of Mount Sinai. He led his people as a shepherd. He warded off enemies, argued with God on their behalf, disciplined them with his staff, and loved them till their last breaths. And Moses died on the mountaintop overlooking Canaan, the land God promised. He made his bed not in the promised land but in an unmarked grave, left to rot by the people he loved dearly. It was a heartbreaking ending to a life well lived.

Epilogue

I often wonder how Moses felt as he took his last few breaths on the mountain. Did he feel as if he threw away his life? If he had the choice, would he have done it another way? Maybe he would have repented to Pharaoh instead of God and remained in Egypt as a prince. Or maybe he would have ignored the burning bush entirely—chalked up the vision to a spoiled breakfast—kept his sandals on his feet, and chased after his sheep. Would he have preferred a quiet death with an ordinary life, tending to sheep and family?

I like to imagine that Moses was calm on his deathbed, breathing peacefully, lips curled, satisfied with the life he lived. He walked with God and gave himself over to something bigger than himself. A good leaving is formed by a good arriving, and vice versa. A person who has arrived with God will know how to leave with God, just as a person who has left with God will always arrive with God. To live in God's prodigal care is to die in God's prodigal care.

Moses was born into a kingdom ruled by a man who spoke death, rather than life, into being. Pharaoh's edict ordered all the male Hebrew babies to be drowned, but Moses's mother thought quickly. She put her baby in a basket, or an ark, and floated him down the Nile River. His vocation began with water and an ark, the trust that God would raise him from infanticide. Pharaoh's daughter found him squealing in the water. She knew he was a Hebrew and saved him anyway. Moses was welcomed by a foreign people and was accepted as one of their own. It's no wonder he later learned to care for a foreign people—the enslaved Hebrew people of his flesh and blood. Moses would later give his life as a nanny to the Israelites, just as his Hebrew midwives served as a nanny to him.

Moses then escaped from Egypt to become a shepherd in Midian—pulled inward by God before he was pushed outward. Tending to his flock, he stumbled upon a burning bush that wasn't consumed. There, Moses learned how to see, gazing into the beautiful and mesmerizing fire.

> *To be received is to receive.*

Teachers have commented that the burning bush is about learning to pay attention, to behold beauty in the most unlikely places. Rabbi

Lawrence Kushner puts it this way: "God wanted to find out whether or not Moses could pay attention to something for more than a few minutes. When Moses did, God spoke. The trick is paying attention to what is happening around you long enough to behold the miracle without falling asleep. There is another world, right here within this one, whenever we pay attention."[1] Moses got used to being surprised by God.

Other rabbis have asked why God chose to speak out of a "lowly thorn bush," which is the Aramaic translation. Why not the palm tree or the olive tree? Here's their answer: Nothing is too insignificant to merit God's attention. God chose the thorn bush to teach us that holiness resides not in high mountains nor towering cedars but in humility. That's a habit Moses would need for the rest of his life; he learned it there as a shepherd in Midian.

The burning bush is a curriculum in beauty: A light that shines in the most mundane, lowly objects.

> *To behold God's beauty is to find God in the most unlikely places.*

Moses would again behold God's beauty even more intimately at the top of Sinai, where he was bold enough to ask to see God's face. "Show me your glory," says Moses. God says, "No. It would be like looking directly at the sun." Instead, God offers a compromise: "Hide in the cleft, I'll walk past, and you can see my backside" (see Exod. 33:18–23). To be clear, "backside" is how your grandmother says "ass." And that's the most any of us could hope for the chance to see God as we follow God. The Israelites, covered in the dust of their God, strain to see their God as they follow the One who blazes the trail ahead of them.

The name that God gave Moses at the burning bush is YHWH. There are no vowels. We're not even sure how to say God's name. Nor are we sure what it means. God's face is too brilliant to be perceived, and God's name is too holy to be pronounced or comprehended. God cannot be controlled; God can only be followed.

Epilogue

> *YHWH.*
> *I Am*
> *causing to*
> *Be who*
> *I will to*
> *Be where*
> *I Am.*
>
> *But*
> *I am not*
> *one who can*
> *talk. And*
> *I am not*
> *the one you want me*
> *to be.*
> *Still, I will go where*
> *You Are*
> *calling.*

God saw the Israelites' pain and raised Moses to lead the people to freedom through the Red Sea by making dry land out of chaos. And so, God led them through a narrow path through the sea. The Israelites emerged from the narrow (*mitzrayim*) life in Egypt, where the walls closed and there was no escape. The irony is that when the Egyptians entered the water, the walls of the water collapsed. Those who try to drown others are likely to be drowned. But those who are set free are called to lead others to freedom. Still today, billions of people have followed Moses through the Red Sea, drowned, and been raised to new life in God.

The Israelites emerged from the water, freed from the bondage of evil and death. But freedom, when first experienced, doesn't always feel like freedom. It feels like death. The wilderness was wide open. How would they know which way to travel? When you're born again, the whole world can feel intimidating.

Moses walked with his people for forty years without a map. It was devastating. The journey shouldn't have taken forty years, much less one year, to get from Egypt to Canaan. The actual distance is about 120 miles. A good Appalachian through-hiker could do it in under a week. These Israelites would have made circles while an entire generation passed away. But the spiritual distance is always longer than the geographical. It might not take forty years to walk from Egypt to Canaan, but it could take at least forty years for your heart to get there—to know your true self and the God who loves you.

Theologian Kosuke Koyama suggests that some things God can teach us only very slowly, at a walking pace. Thankfully, we never walk alone. We always walk with God. Koyama says that God walks three-miles-an-hour because that's the speed of our walking. He writes, "God walks slowly because God is love."[2]

• • • • • • • • • • • • • • • • • • • ✦ • • • • • • • • • • • • • • • • • • •

In most generations, God will use the wilderness to teach us how to be the people of God through simplicity, solitude, and prayer. These are the rhythms of grace. The stars in the sky can only be seen when all the lights are turned off. But when you emerge from the wilderness, you shine so brightly that you can give light to the whole world.

> *To be named by God through water and the spirit is to follow even when the destination is unclear.*

With unlimited directions and unlimited anxiety, the Israelites complained—a lot. And for good reason. I've walked through the Judean wilderness. It's beautiful, but it's not a leisurely hike. It's rugged and mountainous. Food appears to be scarce. Turns out that it was. The Israelites cried, "You led us out of slavery to die! Remember in Egypt? We ate fish—and it was free. That's to say nothing of the cucumbers and melons, the leeks, onions, and garlic" (see Exod. 14:11). Normal is never as good as you remember. The menu in Egypt was toil and strife. Nostalgia is seductive; it tells you what you want to hear but rarely tells the whole truth. More often, it's a half-truth. The Israelites had food in Egypt, but they ate with their hands in shackles.

Epilogue

God, wasteful in grace, refused to rain down thunder and lightning. God bears with them like a parent whose children are whining about what's on the dinner plate. Most often, God's people get what they don't deserve—life. God generously rains bread from heaven. It's profligate. Extravagant. It's table fellowship. And the Israelites begin to rediscover that they can't live out of their means without the God who sustains them.

> *The school of the wilderness teaches community with knives and forks.*

Here's an early Judeo-Christian maxim: Change the eating, change the life. This bread, called manna, was provided each morning for the Israelites to take what they needed and nothing more. Notice the difference. Pharaoh's economy was structured on wealth and accumulation. How much can you store up from the backs of other people? But the economy of God is established on "enough." No one gets too much. And no one gets too little.

The God who creates out of community won't save without community. The Israelites began a new curriculum on redistribution and the common good. The Israelites are led to realize how deeply they are connected and how intertwined their lives are with one another. They can't live alone. What you receive from God can't be hoarded. If you try to hoard it, it will rot. Eat together, conversely, and you will learn to love one another and share true communion.

> *And there was enough— even with time to waste.*

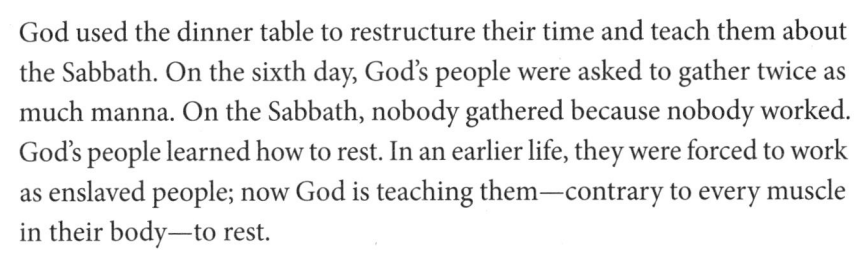

God used the dinner table to restructure their time and teach them about the Sabbath. On the sixth day, God's people were asked to gather twice as much manna. On the Sabbath, nobody gathered because nobody worked. God's people learned how to rest. In an earlier life, they were forced to work as enslaved people; now God is teaching them—contrary to every muscle in their body—to rest.

Finally, Moses stood on the zenith of Mount Tabor and took his last breath. As tragic as it was, Moses's death was shaded by hope. He had seen the promised land. Was Moses denied the promised land as a punishment for striking a rock with a staff at Maribah Kadesh when he should have used his words? There's no clear consensus that Moses was being punished. Like most deaths, the answer isn't simple. Even if there was an answer, it couldn't bring him back out of the grave.

Maybe Moses died because he had given himself away completely as if his life was manna from heaven.

And maybe that's the point of the Judeo-Christian life: If you try to hoard your life, you will rot away. But if you believe that God is in the business of manna, then you know there's always more to hand out. Receive it—all of it—the hospitality, beauty, rest, love. And share it before it rots. Jesus would later make the same case: "Those who find their life will lose it, and those who lose their life for my sake will find it" (Matt. 10:39). Moses's life was not fruitful because he accomplished much, though he did. His life was fruitful because he emptied his life, dying to himself, that he might be filled with God.

The exodus (and the Passover meal commemorating it) is Judaism's foundation. The Jewish people gather around a table every year to share food and wine. A child will ask, "How is tonight unlike any other night?" They tell the story. The story tells them who they are: a people freed from slavery. Remember when we went camping with God? We were under the stars for forty years. That's where God put us on the potter's wheel and formed us to be humans and not enslaved people. The exodus is a prototype for all the people of God in every generation; it's the fundamental spiritual story of what God is constantly doing. Rabbi Nachman of Breslov said, "The Exodus from Egypt occurs in every human being, in every era, in every year, and in every day."[3] God is constantly taking narrow places and widening them, whether it's nations, people, or hearts.

> *He gave it away—all of it—extravagantly, wastefully.*

Epilogue

Moses's life encapsulates everything we have covered thus far: extravagant hospitality, beauty in the most dismal circumstances, the shaping and reshaping of time, and a vocation of creation and growth in holiness. This is to say that Moses's life was a life of worship—a life that makes no sense apart from God and God's dream for the world. He took a leap of faith in the face of fear and then took another, witnessing to the hope that God would never let him fall without being caught.

Everything we need to know about the Christian life is there in the life of Moses, as Jesus gives us eyes to see. As Christians, our life with Christ begins with the splitting and the crossing of the Red Sea—our baptism—where we are re-created, are set free, and enter into solidarity with God and a new community. In the Red Sea, we drown the Egyptian (or every form of evil) and rise clothed in Christ. Our lives of slavery, to sin and death, have been left behind. We start the journey toward the land that God has promised.

> *To tell the story is to become the story.*

Then, we enter the wilderness. It's the middle of our lives, sandwiched between our slavery and the promised land. The middle can be frightening, full of wandering, death, doubt, and fear. It feels like it takes longer than it should. But God is present—on the mountains and in the valleys. We learn to take off our sandals and dwell at the foot of every burning bush.

In the middle, we gather at the table to eat, to learn the table manners for a new economy. Time is kept differently. The clock is not so much a slave master as it is a gift. And time is not infinite, but nor is it in short supply. There is enough to gather around dinner tables and share the manna, the sustenance we need every day, to tell and receive stories. God saves through the community that gathers to tell the story, shares a meal, and carries that love into the world.

There will come a time when you'll climb up a mountain, and you won't walk down. A final stranger, the angel of death, will show up at our door. But we'll realize that this angel is no stranger after all. The life given to God is steeped in training for our own deaths. A life of worship is spent dying to self to be raised by God. Finally, when there's nothing left to give, you'll hand over your last breath and take a step into one final wilderness. Our lives will end, not like a thief in the night but a final note in one of God's most beautiful symphonies.

The good news is that you've already been shown the promised land—it's resurrection. The condition of not fearing exits is shaped by the hope that there is always another entrance. There is a final arrival, a one-way road into God's everlasting arms, and a final chapter that will not end. The future is good because the future is in God. And God has chosen not to be God without you. You are a part of God's story—eternally. And because God's story never ends, yours won't either.

When we walk through the final door, we will be joined by all of the other water molecules in the Jordan River, where all sin dies, and holiness is raised. We are a sentence, a word, a comma in an eternal story. We are, maybe, a note in the song God is singing or a drop of paint on the canvas God is painting. We are but one grape and one grain of wheat in a chalice and loaf of bread at the table of the Lord. Together, we join hands at the table for a never-ending feast.

At the end of all things, will I believe that I have wasted my life?

I hope so.

> *May the peace of the Lord Christ go with you,*
> *wherever He may send you.*
> *May He guide you through the wilderness,*
> *protect you through the storm.*
> *May He bring you home, rejoicing*
> *at the wonders He has shown you.*
> *May He bring you home, rejoicing*
> *once again into our doors.*

ACKNOWLEDGMENTS

Bellwood and Spiller Park West, I wrote 75 percent of this in your spaces. Thanks for the vibes and caffeine.

The Survivors, for talking me off the ledge.

Backyardigans, AJC, few people took the time to read drafts.

ACC and Derek, Anne Lamott tells a story of getting lost as a kid. A police officer picked her up, and they drove around until Anne spotted her church. She knew she could get home from there.

N&K, for keeping the cellar open.

Sniders and MacMinns, for the zim zum.

E&P, for quiet Saturday mornings. I owe you a game of hide and seek.

Jason and ACU Press, for making my work stronger.

D, you're my best friend, the other half of my heart. Thanks for showing me what true friendship looks like. You are every cliché: a rock, a light, a fortress. Let's get a heart necklace from Claire's.

NOTES

Prelude

[1] This is Norman Wirzba's phrase.

[2] Here, I am influenced by James K. A. Smith, *Desiring the Kingdom: Worship, Worldview, and Cultural Formation* (Grand Rapids: Baker Academic, 2009).

[3] See Tony Campolo, *Who Switched the Price Tags?* (Nashville: Thomas Neslon, 2008).

[4] David Foster Wallace, *This Is Water: Some Thoughts, Delivered on a Significant Occasion, about Living a Compassionate Life* (New York: Little, Brown and Company, 2009), 98–106.

[5] J. Aaron Simmons, *Camping with Kierkegaard: Faithfulness as a Way of Life* (Wisdom/Work, 2023), 15.

[6] Dietrich Bonhoeffer, *Worldly Preaching: Lectures on Homiletics*, ed. and trans. Clyde E. Fant (New York: Thomas Nelson, 1975), 126.

[7] This is Henri Nouwen's language.

You Have Been Welcomed

[1] Augustine, *Confessions*, 11.12.262.

[2] Jürgen Moltmann, "The Origin and Completion of Time in the Primordial and in the Eschatological Moment," in *Science and Wisdom*, trans. M. Kohl (Minneapolis: Fortress, 2003), 114.

[3] Matthew Fox, *Meditations with Meister Eckhart* (Santa Fe: Bear & Company, 1983), 129.

Embraced by Family and Friends

[1] Robert Frost, "The Death of the Hired Man," in *North of Boston* (London: David Nutt, 1914).

[2] Henri Nouwen, *Reaching Out: The Three Movements of the Spiritual Life* (New York: Doubleday, 1966), 81.

[3] Quoted in Christine Pohl, *Making Room: Recovering Hospitality as a Christian Tradition* (Grand Rapids: Eerdmans, 1999), 172-73.

[4] This is Søren Kierkegaard's phrase.

[5] Rosaria Butterfield, *The Gospel Comes with a House Key: Practicing Radically Ordinary Hospitality in Our Post-Christian World* (Wheaton, IL: Crossway Publishing, 2018).

[6] See the overarching argument of Samuel Wells in *A Nazareth Manifesto: Being with God* (Chichester, West Sussex: John Wiley & Sons, 2015).

[7] Augustine, *Confessions* 4.4.7.

[8] Augustine, *Confessions* 4.6.11.

[9] Aristotle, *Nichomachean Ethics*, trans. J. A. K. Thomson (London: Penguin Books, 2004), 200.

[10] Karl Barth, *Church Dogmatics* 2.1, ed. G. W. Bromiley and T. F. Torrance (New York: Charles Scribner's Sons, 1957).

[11] Jacques Derrida, "Hostipitality," *Angelaki* 5, no. 3 (2000): 3-18.

[12] C. S. Lewis, *The Four Loves* (1960; reprint, Boston: Mariner Books, 2012), 156.

[13] J. R. R. Tolkien, *The Fellowship of the Ring* (New York: Mifflin Harcourt Publishing, 1954), 103.

[14] Lewis, *Four Loves*, 92.

At Home in Body and Spirit

[1] Henri Nouwen, *Reaching Out: The Three Movements of the Spiritual Life* (New York: Doubleday, 1966), 66.

[2] See Samuel Wells, "A Criminal Waste," Duke University Chapel at Duke University, Durham, NC, March 14, 2010.

Singing Is Who We Are

[1] Mary Oliver, *Blue Horses: Poems* (New York: Penguin Press, 2014), 25.

[2] Jeremy Begbie, *Resounding Truth: Christian Wisdom in the World of Music* (Grand Rapids: Baker Academic, 2007), 15.

[3] Walter Brueggemann, *The Psalms and the Life of Faith* (Minneapolis: Fortress Press, 1995), 24.

[4] Kathleen Norris, *Dakota: A Spiritual Geography* (1993; reprint, Boston: Mariner Books, 2001), 91.

Cross-Shaped Pictures

[1] Jurgen Moltmann, *The Living God and the Fullness of Life* (Louisville: Westminster John Knox Press), 166.

[2] Ludwig Wittgenstein, *Philosophical Investigations*, trans. G. E. M. Anscombe (Oxford: Basil Blackwell, 1958), 31.

[3] Joseph Ratzinger, "The Feeling of Things, the Contemplation of Beauty" (August 24, 2002); Benedict XVI, Meeting with Artists (November 21, 2009).

[4] Barth, *Church Dogmatics* 2.1, 665.

[5] Carl Jung, *Memories, Dreams, Reflections*, trans. Richard and Clara Winston (New York: Vintage Books, 1963), 355.

[6] Barbara Brown Taylor, "Sermon at the Palma Ceia Presbyterian Church," Tampa, Florida, April 22, 2018, http://www.nicoleabdnour.com/blog/guest-post-sermon-by-barbara-brown-taylor.

Singing Who We Will Be

[1] Friedrich Nietzsche, *Thus Spake Zarathustra*, trans. Thomas Common (Overland Park, KS: Digireads.com Publishing, 2016), 75.

[2] Andrew Fletcher, "An Account of a Conversation concerning a Right Regulation of Government for the Good of Mankind. In a Letter to the Marquis of Montrose" (1704), quoted in Susan Ratcliffe, ed., *Oxford Essential Quotations*, 4th ed., online version (Oxford: Oxford University Press, 2016).

[3] See Rollo May, *The Courage to Create* (New York: Norton & Company, 1994), 68.

[4] May, *Courage to Create*, 56.

[5] Herbert Marcuse, *The Aesthetic Dimension: Toward a Critique of Marxist Aesthetics* (Boston: Beacon Press, 1978), 9.

[6] Reggie L. Williams, *Bonhoeffer's Black Jesus: Harlem Renaissance Theology and an Ethic of Resistance* (Waco, TX: Baylor University Press, 2021), 26.

[7] Marcuse, *Aesthetic Dimension*, 32.

[8] See Charles Campbell, "Sermon," May 11, 2019, Duke Divinity School's 93rd Baccalaureate, Duke University, Durham, NC, https://chapel.duke.edu/events/duke-divinity-schools-93rd-baccalaureate-1557613800-1557619200.

[9] See Samuel Wells, "Living on the Edge," October 17, 2015, St. Martin in the Fields, London, England, https://www.inclusive-church.org/wp-content/uploads/2020/05/Living-on-the-Edge-Sam-Wells.pdf.

A Genesis

[1] Alasdair MacIntyre, *After Virtue: A Study in Moral Theory*, 3rd ed. (Notre Dame: University of Notre Dame Press, 1981), 216.

[2] Flannery O'Connor, *A Prayer Journal* (New York: Farrar, Straus and Giroux, 2013).

[3] Søren Kierkegaard, *Attack Upon "Christendom,"* trans. Walter Lowrie (Princeton: Princeton University Press, 1968), 150.

[4] Stephen Backhouse, *Kierkegaard: A Single Life* (Grand Rapids: Zondervan, 2016), 296

[5] Hans Adolph Brorson, "Halleluja, jeg har min Jesum funden [Hallelujah, I have found my Jesus]," hymn in *Troens rare Klenodie (The Rare Treasure of Faith)*, 1739.

[6] C. S. Lewis, *The Lion, the Witch, and the Wardrobe*, illus. Pauline Baynes (New York: HarperCollins, 1950), 47

[7] C. S. Lewis, *The Voyage of the Dawn Treader* (Grand Rapids: Zondervan, 2000), 156–57.

Seventy Faces of the Torah

[1] Sam Wells, *Improvisation: The Drama of Christian Ethics* (Grand Rapids: Brazos Press, 2004).

[2] See Karl Barth, *The Word of God and the Word of Man*, ed. and trans. Douglas Horton (Cleveland, OH: Pilgrim Press, 1928), 28–50.

[3] This is Willie Jennings's story. I heard him tell it in class when I was a divinity student at Duke.

[4] Annie Dillard, "Holy the Firm," in *The Annie Dillard Reader* (New York: HarperPerennial, 1995), 446–47.

[5] *Bamidbar Rabbah* 13:14.

[6] Mishnah, *Pirkei Avot* 5:22.

Touching the Gospel

[1] Gregory of Nazianzus to Cledonius the Presbyter, "Letter 101."

[2] C. S. Lewis, *The Four Loves* (1960; reprint, New York: Houghton Mifflin Harcourt, 1991), 90.

[3] See Don Golden and Rob Bell, *Jesus Wants to Save Christians: Learning to Read a Dangerous Book* (Grand Rapids: HarperOne, 2014).

The Longest, Shortest Time

[1] Jouvenal, *Satire* 10.77–81.

[2] James Boswell, *The Life of Samuel Johnson*, 2nd ed., vol. 2 (1791; New York: Harper, 1846), 118.

[3] See Hartmut Rosa, *Social Acceleration: A New Theory of Modernity*, trans. Jonathan Trejo-Mathys (New York: Columbia University Press, 2013).

[4] Andy Root, *The Congregation in a Secular Age* (Grand Rapids: Baker Academic, 2021), 67.

[5] Augustine, *Confessions*, trans. Henry Chadwick (Oxford: Oxford University Press, 1998), 11.25.32.

Evening, Morning—A Day

[1] Eugene Peterson, "The Good for Nothing Sabbath," *Christianity Today*, April 5, 1994, 34–37.

A Week

[1] James K. A. Smith, *How to Inhabit Time: Understanding the Past, Facing the Future, and Living Faithfully Now* (Grand Rapids: Brazos Press, 2022), 1.

[2] Abraham Joshua Heschel, *The Sabbath* (1951; New York: Farrar, Straus, and Giroux, 2005), 10.

[3] Peterson, "The Good for Nothing Sabbath," 34–37.

[4] Smith, *How to Inhabit Time*, 85.

[5] Mary Oliver, *West Wind: Poems and Prose Poems* (Boston: Mariner Books, 1997), 3.
[6] This is Ryan Bonfiglio's observation.
[7] Walter Brueggemann, *Sabbath as Resistance: Saying No to the Culture of Now* (Louisville, KY: Westminster John Knox Press, 2014), 42.
[8] Breuggemann, *Sabbath as Resistance*, 27.
[9] *The Cloud of Unknowing*, ed. Bernard Bangley (Brewster, MA: Paraclete Press: 2009), 7.
[10] Anne Lamott, *Almost Everything: Notes on Hope* (New York: Riverhead Books, 2018), 67.
[11] Henri Nouwen, *Turn My Mourning into Dancing: Finding Hope in Hard Times* (Nashville: W Publishing, 2001), 9.
[12] C. S. Lewis, *Yours, Jack: Spiritual Direction from C. S. Lewis* (New York: Harper Collins, 2008), 97-98.

Setting the Table

[1] A version of this chapter appears in Ryan Snider, "Politics of the Table," *Agape Review*, December 20, 2021, https://agapereview.com/2021/12/20/politicsofthetable/. Used with permission.
[2] Mary Douglas, "The Forbidden Animals in Leviticus," *Journal for the Study of the Old Testament* 18, no. 59 (Sep. 1993): 21-23.
[3] Lauren Winner, *Mudhouse Sabbath: An Invitation to a Life of Spiritual Discipline* (Brewster, MA: Paraclete Press, 2007), 17.
[4] Stanley Hauerwas, "Christian Practice and the Practice of Law in a World Without Foundations," *Mercer Law Review* 44, no. 3 (1993): 750.

Thanksgiving

[1] These are the words of the Modeh Ani, a Jewish prayer that dates back to the seventeenth century.
[2] Martin Luther King Jr., "Christmas Sermon on Peace," aired December 24, 1967, YouTube video, https://www.youtube.com/watch?v=1jeyIAH3bUI.
[3] Norman Wirzba, *Food and Faith: A Theology of Eating* (Cambridge, UK: Cambridge University Press, 2011), 198.
[4] Wirzba, *Food and Faith*, 197.

Anamnesis

[1] *Didache* 9:4, trans. Aaron Milavec, *The Didache: Text, Translation, Analysis, and Commentary* (Collegeville, MN: Liturgical Press, 2003).
[2] John F. Desmond, "Flannery O'Connor and the Symbol," *Logos: A Journal of Catholic Thought and Culture* 5, no. 2 (2002): 143-56.
[3] John Howard Yoder, *Body Politics: Five Practices of the Christian Community before the Watching World* (Scottsdale, PA: Herald Press, 1992), 16.

[4] Augustine writes, "I am the food of the fully grown; grow and you will feed on me. And you will not change me into the food your flesh eats, but you will be changed into me." *Confessions* 7.10.16.

Take, Bless, Break, Give

[1] Willie Jennings used this language in a class.

[2] Norman Wirzba, *Food and Faith: A Theology of Eating* (Cambridge, UK: Cambridge University Press, 2011), 158.

[3] Sam Wells, "Teaching Eucharist," Duke Divinity School Chapel, September 20, 2009.

A Baptism

[1] Chris Green, *Being Transfigured: Lenten Homilies* (Abbotsford, BC: St Macrina Press, 2023), 32.

Confession of Doubt

[1] Óscar Romero, *The Church Is All of You: Thoughts of Archbishop Oscar Romero*, comp. and trans. James R. Brockton (London: Collins Fount Paperbacks, 1985), 90.

[2] This quotation is part of the Augustine legacy, but the actual source of this quote is unknown.

[3] Søren Kierkegaard, *Fear and Trembling/Repetition*, ed. and trans. Howard V. Hong and Edna H. Hong (Princeton: Princeton University Press, 1983), 65.

[4] Julian Barnes, *Nothing to Be Frightened Of* (Toronto, Ontario: Vintage Canada, 2009), 1.

[5] For a fuller discussion of the fragility of belief and truth, see Charles Taylor, *A Secular Age* (Cambridge, MA: Belknap Press, 2009).

[6] Dietrich Bonhoeffer, *Theological Education Underground: 1937–1940*, ed. Victoria J. Barnett, trans. Victoria J. Barnett, Claudia D. Bergmann, Peter Frick, and Scott A. Moore (Minneapolis: Fortress, 2012), 476–80.

[7] Paul Ricoeur, *The Symbolism of Evil* (Boston: Beacon Press, 1967).

[8] Flannery O'Connor, *The Complete Stories* (New York: Farrar, Straus and Giroux, 1971), 477.

[9] Lauren Winner, *Still: Notes on a Mid-Faith Crisis* (San Francisco: HarperOne, 2012), 172.

Prayer

[1] Mother Teresa, *Come Be My Light: The Private Writings of the "Saint of Calcutta,"* ed. Brian Kolodiejchuk (Waterville, ME: Wheeler, 2008), 316.

[2] Ricky Gervais (@rickygervais), X, May 21, 2013, 7:51 a.m., https://twitter.com/rickygervais/status/336856739800571905?lang=en.

[3] Madeleine L'Engle, *Two Part Invention: The Story of a Marriage* (San Francisco: HarperOne, 1989), 193–94.

[4] *Cyclopedia of Religious Anecdotes*, compiled by James Gilchrist Lawson (New York: Fleming H. Revell Company, 1923), 303.

Notes

Watching the Tides

[1] Thomas Merton, *Thoughts in Solitude* (1958; reprint, New York: Farrar, Straux, Giroux, 1999), 79.

Following God's (Ordinary) Call

[1] Søren Kierkegaard, *The Concept of Anxiety*, trans. Alastair Hannay (New York: Liverlight, 2014), 188.

[2] Kierkegaard, *Concept of Anxiety*, 193.

[3] Frederick Buechner, *Wishful Thinking: A Seeker's ABC* (New York: HarperOne, 1993), 118–19.

[4] John Steinbeck, *East of Eden* (New York: Penguin Books, 2016), 302.

[5] Barbara Brown Taylor, *An Altar in the World: A Geography of Faith* (New York: HarperOne, 2009), 112.

[6] Tony Campolo, *Let Me Tell You a Story: Life Lessons from Unexpected Places and Unlikely People* (Nashville: Thomas Nelson, 2000), 144–45.

[7] Augustine, *Confessions* 6.6.9.

[8] Saint Francis, the son of a wealthy cloth merchant and landowner, heard God calling him to "rebuild the church." He renounced everything his father had given him, even the expensive clothes on his back, stripped naked in the town square, and followed Jesus. There is no evidence that his father would talk to him again.

[9] Lesslie Newbigin, *The Gospel in a Pluralist Society* (Grand Rapids: Eerdmans, 1989), 11.

Planted in New Soil

[1] G. K. Chesterton, *What's Wrong with the World* (New York: Dodd, Mead, and Company, 1912), 48.

[2] Christine Pohl, *Making Room: Recovering Hospitality as a Christian Tradition* (Grand Rapids: Eerdmans, 1999), 43–44.

[3] Jason Byassee planted this seed. *The Gifts of the Small Church: Ministry in the Small Membership Church* (Nashville: Abingdon Press, 2010).

[4] Henri Nouwen, *Reaching Out: The Three Movements of the Spiritual Life* (New York: Doubleday, 1966), 53.

[5] This is Norman Wirzba's language.

[6] Wendell Berry, *A Timbered Choir: The Sabbath Poems* (Berkeley, CA: Counterpoint, 1998), 131.

Epilogue

[1] Lawrence Kushner, *God Was in This Place and I, i Did Not Know: Finding Self, Spirituality, and Ultimate Meaning* (Woodstock, VT: Jewish Lights, 1993), 25.

[2] Kosuke Koyama, *Three Mile an Hour God* (Maryknoll, NY: Orbit, 1980), 7.

[3] Rabbi Nachman (1771–1822) revived the Hasidic movement in Ukraine.